Praise for *Do It, Mean It, Be It*

"One of the best and most practical books yet. Learn how to purposefully plan your career and integrate it with your personal goals and aspirations."
—James Scriven, CEO, Inter-American Investment Corporation

"With her widely recognized expertise, and ability to communicate with both humor and insight, Corrie lays out well the keys to succeeding in business and your career while living a life that is meaningful and worthwhile."
—Caroline Goldie, Chief Strategy Officer, IFC, World Bank Group

DO IT
MEAN IT
BE IT

The Keys to Achieve Success, Happiness, and Everything You Deserve at Work and in Life

CORRIE SHANAHAN

The Career Press, Inc.
Wayne, NJ

Do It, Mean It, Be It
Typeset by PerfecType, Nashville, Tennessee
Cover design by Joanna Williams
Printed in the U.S.A.

To order this title, please call toll-free 1-800-CAREER-1 (NJ and Canada: 201-848-0310) to order using VISA or MasterCard, or for further information on books from Career Press.

The Career Press, Inc.
12 Parish Drive
Wayne, NJ 07470
www.careerpress.com

Library of Congress Cataloging-in-Publication Data

CIP Data Available Upon Request.

For my darling boy, Sam,
with all my love

Bernie,

Fabulous to
hang out with
you guys!
Congrats on the
next phase —

Connie

ACKNOWLEDGMENTS

There are so many people without whom this book would never have seen the light of day. Thank you to Alan Weiss and his community of intrepid consultants who gave me the inspiration for the book, made me so welcome, and were so generous and kind. Thank you to the people who have influenced me along the way, including Robert and Rosalind Fritz; Paul Spain, Michael Nolan and my friends at Sheppard Moscow; Bruce Moats, Lisa Kopp, and all my friends and colleagues at IFC and the World Bank. Thanks to Marshall Goldsmith, Elizabeth Littlefield, Bruce McNamer, Jenny Scott, Lars Thunell, and Elizabeth Vazquez who generously gave their time to be featured in a leader profile.

Thanks to my girlfriends, without whom this life would have been so much poorer, Caitriona Palmer, Caroline Sergeant, Caroline Goldie, Lisa Greenman, Tania Banotti, Helen Loughman, Olga Harrington, Tesa Conlin, Caroline Robb, Corinne Figueredo, Amanda Ellis, Maria Pedersen, Mary Challinor, Jean Duff, Kelly Widelska, Evelyn Farkas, Dorothy Berry, and many others. I have been blessed in my neighbors and friends. I'm grateful to Alvaro and Janice, who always took me in. I have also been blessed in my family, my mother and brother Neal,and my darling sister Barbara, who is also a best friend. And most of all, I have been blessed to know and love my son, Sam Beesley, "The best boy any mother could ever have had."

CONTENTS

INTRODUCTION

Why I Wrote This Book

I wrote this book because I was frustrated by the number of people who are unhappy with their lives. Too many friends and colleagues complained about hating their jobs, feeling overwhelmed, and not doing the things they really enjoyed. They reported being anxious about their careers, money, relationships, and their lives in general. External events, such as the aftermath of the global financial crisis, the rise of extremism, mass shootings, terror attacks, and Brexit didn't help. The doom and fear-mongering seemed to increase with each new attack and piece of bad economic news. It felt like uncertainty and anxiety had become permanent states.

But I don't buy that. I believe that life is rich and good, and it should be lived fully. A couple of years ago I left the relative safety of corporate life to fulfill my dream of having my own business. I love being an entrepreneur. Sure, it is hard work, but it is also extremely satisfying and fun. Every day I help senior executives reach their goals in business and in life. A bout of cancer and accompanying brush with death this year helped confirm the choices I had made. I was reminded why I like my life so much. Those events made me think more about why people don't live the lives they want and how I could help them. If I can gather some of the wisdom I have gained working with my clients, why not share it and make it available to others?

What This Book Can Do for You

This book will help you clarify what is really important to you, it will help you identify the things you want to change, and it will give you all the practical tools to get there. I cover everything from home and work, in between, and beyond.

You'll learn to be much more proactive in creating your ideal life. You will learn how to build a system to support your goals. You will also learn how to enjoy and maintain your new state.

Whether you want to jump-start your career, grow a new business, or figure out how to work less and spend more time with the people you love, you'll find the tools to do that in this book.

The Best Ways to Use This Book

Quickly read the book all the way through. Then, go back and start doing the exercises in the areas you care about most. That might include setting goals, getting support infrastructure, or building your brand at work. This book includes real-life examples from around the world from senior figures in business, politics, and the arts that can help and inspire you.

You'll hear from people who have shared what worked for them, how they got where they are today, and built the life they wanted. It is chock-full of practical exercises and checklists that will help you focus and jump-start the ability to find happiness in your life, at work, and in the world. Do it. Mean it. Be it. No more procrastinating or complaining. This is all you need to get started on the road to a happier, more successful, and more enjoyable life.

You Already Won the Lottery

I n a nutshell: First of all, congratulate yourself. You're doing something right. You must be doing something right to even be reading this book. You have been successful in your career and are ambitious to do even better. Sure, things are not perfect; maybe you're even going through a particularly challenging phase in your professional or private life right now. But if you're reading this, you're probably better off than the four billion people on the planet living on less than $2 per day. Sometimes it helps to count our blessings.

Count Your Blessings

Counting your blessings helps to put things in perspective. What am I grateful for? What went well today? A number of years ago I had dinner for the first time at the home of a new friend. She was a senior official in the Obama administration and her husband was an expert in environmental issues for a large bank. They were a blended family with two teenage boys and a couple of dogs. Busy lives, busy careers. What struck me that first evening at family dinner was their habit of asking everyone at the table what they were thankful for. It wasn't a special occasion, just a regular weeknight. It was simply what they did whenever they had dinner together.

We went around the table and each said what we were thankful for. I felt slightly awkward, but no one else did. Each person took his or her turn. I said I was thankful to be there and to be part of their family for the evening. I've since made that a habit in my own home, both when we gather with friends, and each weekday night my son and I sit down to eat dinner together. It's a powerful but simple way to reflect on how fortunate we are.

Martin Seligman, at the University of Pennsylvania, is considered the father of positive psychology: the philosophy that we should build on our strengths, rather than fret about fixing our weaknesses. In his book *Flourish*,[1] he recommends a somewhat similar exercise called "What went well, and why." Here is how it works: At your dinner table, ask people what went well in their day or week and follow up by asking why. This helps your friends or family members to fully recall the good things they experienced and what led to them. You can also do this as a journal exercise at night before going to sleep. I can't vouch for the neuroscience behind it, but I can tell you from experience that recalling positive events and describing them to others is a very effective way of improving your mood and well-being.

Another simple way to count your blessings is to look around you. You don't have to go to the poorest countries in the world to see that you are better off than most people on the planet. In your own city or community there are many people who lack the things you take for granted or who have been devastated by loss. Even when you face serious challenges with your health, finances, or relationships, chances are you're still better off than many. You likely have access to resources and the support of others to help you deal with difficult circumstances as you go through a challenging time.

Right now, jot down a list of all the things you have to be thankful for. Don't forget to start with the basics of food, shelter, and companionship. Keep adding. You'll find it's a long list. (You may want to get a journal to use with this book, as there will be lots of exercises like this with notes you'll want to return to.)

What Got You Here

We are often so focused on what's missing or could be better in our lives that we forget to take stock of what's working. We skip over what we do well and beat ourselves up about what we do poorly. It's time for a little inventory. Instead of waiting for your annual performance appraisal, do one on yourself right now. What are your greatest strengths? What do you do really well? What do people most appreciate about you?

Exercise: *Create two columns and jot down your greatest strengths and your greatest achievements. Make sure to include both personal and professional attributes and accomplishments.*

These are the things that got you where you are today. In the achievements column, did you include relationships, friendships, and children? Were you the first person in your family to go to college or start their own business? Maybe you were the first to get a PhD or be worth a million dollars. Do you earn more than your parents ever did?

When we focus on our strengths, we are reminded of what we can do and how far we have come. Sometimes it's very far.

Gary Cohn is the director of the United States Economic Council and the former chief operating officer of Goldman Sachs. He cut a familiar figure on Wall Street, a burly guy with a bald head and ready smile. He was a member of the board of directors of the Institute of International Finance when I was a member of the Institute's management team. He always brought a great energy to boardroom meetings and our events. Gary is very sharp and has been enormously successful. He's also been very open about being dyslexic. In his best-seller *David and Goliath: Underdogs, Misfits, and the Art of Battling Giants*, Malcolm Gladwell recounts Gary's experiences as a child.[2] It took several painful years of teachers thinking he was stupid before he was diagnosed. Gary now credits his dyslexia with his success. He says he got better at taking risks and looking for the upside in opportunities as they arose.

Ironically, our deficits can sometimes be what make us most successful.

Whatever traits you listed as strengths have helped get you to where you are now. Those are the same traits that you will tap into to propel yourself forward and create a more satisfying life.

It's also important to take stock of what you really enjoy about your life currently. What's working well? What do you really love to do? What are the best moments in your week?

For many years, I believed I was trapped in Washington, D.C. My husband and I divorced when my son Sam was very young. Technically, I was free to leave the city, but I wouldn't be able to take Sam with me. His dad was remarried and happily settled in Maryland. He had made it clear he would oppose any move by me to take Sam out of the area. More importantly, they had a good relationship and saw each other frequently.

As Sam got older and his departure to college became more imminent, my options for moving became more of a reality. But then it dawned on me that I had actually built a great life in D.C. and was part of a wonderful community of friends and network of professional relationships. I was too busy looking at grass I thought was greener to realize that I was actually knee-deep in clover!

Exercise: *Take stock now of all the good things in your life and the routines and pleasures you currently enjoy. This list might include your home, neighborhood, favorite exercise class, the route of your favorite run, a regular sports night, a book club, your Saturday routine with friends or children, your summer vacation, and so on.*

Played to Extreme

Your strengths are what got you here, but they can also be what hold you back. When our strengths are overused or misapplied, they can harm us. This is what I call "played to extreme." It's why no one should ever fumble the classic interview question, "What's your greatest weakness?" Don't cite working too hard. That's so obviously self-serving. Instead, take your greatest strength and flip it around. For example, if one of your strengths is attention to detail, then a weakness is likely to be seeking perfection. In other words, paying too much attention to detail. If you continually revise a document before handing it in, or spend more time giving feedback on someone else's work than they spent writing it, you are being self-defeating. You're allowing your strength—attention to detail—to reduce your efficiency.

You've heard the phrase "generous to a fault" to describe someone who is overly generous to the point of harming his or her own self-interest. We see the same in people who have an over-developed tendency to help others and try to provide unsolicited help and advice to the frustration of the recipient. Parents are notably guilty of this one. Ask any teenager!

It's not hard to figure out our greatest weaknesses. Think of feedback you've received in performance appraisals, including all those things with which you didn't agree. Look at the arguments you've had in close relationships. What did the other person accuse you of always doing? Regardless of the merit of their complaint, there's likely some truth there. And, of course, you can go back to your list of strengths and simply exaggerate them to find your weaknesses.

Exercise: *Write down your greatest weaknesses. See if you can find three to five traits or behaviors that regularly land you in trouble.*

Look for patterns in your behavior. There are always one-off circumstances that contribute to something not working out. But if the same thing keeps happening over and over, you become the constant in the equation and you need to look at your own behavior to see what can be changed.

I had an executive coaching client with a demanding job who complained that she worked endless hours cleaning up other people's work. Her team and other colleagues kept handing in sub-par work that she would initially send back to be revised, but eventually fix herself because that was faster. Guess what? They kept submitting sub-par work—until she realized that she needed to change her behavior or nothing was going to change.

A propensity to please can also land you in trouble. If you tend to overcommit and agree with the requests that others make of you, you'll find yourself constantly running and never feeling like you're doing the things that really matter to you.

Laura was a successful writer and journalist who had an alarmingly strong tendency to please. Nothing gave her greater pleasure than other people's gratitude and admiration for her ability to manage tough assignments. No

matter the deadline or difficulty of the writing assignment, she could spin gold from straw and deliver a cred-
ible article in an amazingly short period of time.

She was regularly asked to turn turgid NGO jargon
into compelling case studies that would inspire donors
to fund worthwhile projects in developing countries. She
managed all this from her dining room home office in
Seattle.

However, Laura realized that the more she delivered and the more difficult the assignment, the less it was
regarded as something extraordinary and the more she
found herself working late or slammed against unreason-
able deadlines that left her stressed and anxious. When
she stepped back and realized her strength as a crack
reporter and her desire to please her editors was now
working against her, she was able to push back and start
dictating the terms of how she would work.

How are your strengths working against you? What
bad habits stand in your way of living the life you want?

Michelangelo

Michelangelo was one of the most important artists of the
High Renaissance. An artist, sculptor, architect, and poet,
he's had a lasting impact on artists to this day. Hundreds
of tourists flock to Italy every year to marvel at his paint-
ing in the Sistine Chapel, his *Pietà* depicting Madonna
and Christ, and his statue of David. He is less recognized

for his philosophy, but his thinking around the creative process contains useful lessons for all of us.

If people knew how hard I had to work to gain my mastery, it would not seem so wonderful at all.
—Michelangelo

Michelangelo recognized the importance of hard work, discipline, and effort in honing his craft and creating his masterpieces. He was of the school of "practice makes perfect," not the school of "wait for the muse to strike."

This applies to us in the workplace and our lives as we try to create the life we want to be living, rather than the frazzled, unsatisfying one we've got.

The fastest way to do this is to build upon your strengths. You are not a remedial case. You've had success and done well. This is about building on success and paring away the rest.

Dean Robinson was the head of an accounting firm in Australia that specialized in privately held family businesses. He was excellent at what he did and his clients loved him, but he wasn't happy. He had a team of 15 people, including a partner in the firm with much less experience than him. Dean was the rainmaker, the dealmaker, and the person responsible for quality control. He was unhappy because he was working all hours, constantly fighting fires on the personnel front, and leading a rear guard action to maintain the quality he wanted for his clients.

Although the firm had revenues of $2 million annually, he was only taking home a small portion. He began to resent his employees who were much less committed to the firm than he was and seemed to have a sense of entitlement around pay and benefits that didn't align with their contribution or quality of work.

What Dean really loved about his job was advising clients on their businesses and long-term goals, not the minutiae of their tax returns. He was helping family-owned businesses professionalize, aggressively grow their businesses, and think about the future with succession planning. His clients loved his strategic perspective and the tremendous value it created for their businesses. But Dean was still caught up in the day-to-day dealings of tax returns and audits, not able to offer his strategic services to every client that wanted them. Finally, he decided he had enough.

It had become very clear that Dean's greatest strength was his ability to develop a strategic vision for his clients' businesses and show them how that supported and developed the owner's family life. Yes, he could offer excellent accounting and tax service, but so could others. However, very few people could help family-owned businesses reach their full potential. And that was also what he loved to do.

The greater danger for most of us lies not in setting our aim too high and falling short; but in setting our aim too low, and achieving our mark.
—Michelangelo

So Dean dissolved the partnership, sold the existing practice to his partner, and set out on his own. It took courage, belief in himself, and a lot of discipline and effort to start over, almost from scratch. He was now focused only on what he was best at and discarded the rest.

Dean says the greatest challenges were operational and personal. It was hard on the people around him, including his wife ,who also worked in the business.

"I was having the professional equivalent of a midlife crisis, except for me it wasn't a crisis at all. It was the morphing of a caterpillar into the butterfly," Dean told me. "Some days were awful. I was getting frustrated. I was becoming short-tempered. But I continued to question. I didn't stop and accept what was happening. I did what I had to do to get the task finished and figure out what I could learn and how to do it faster. I am on the right path and know this is what I want to be doing with my life."

I saw the angel in the marble and carved until I set him free. —Michelangelo

There were moments of frustration and anxiety as Dean began to build his new business, but there were no moments of doubt. He knew his strengths and the direction in which he needed to go. You can do the same.

Every block of stone has a statue inside it, and it is the task of the sculptor to discover it. —Michelangelo

Down to the Essentials

In order to create a meaningful life, you need to stop doing some of the things you've been doing up until now, not just begin building new habits. You have to identify the habits, relationships, and beliefs that are holding you back. Then you need to ditch them. Like Michelangelo, you need to pare back what is extraneous to your goal, the life you want. Only then can you live your life in a satisfying, rewarding way.

Easier said than done, right? Take a look right now at where your time is spent.

Exercise: *Keep a journal to track where your time is going. Don't try to account for every task, rather note what you are doing in 15-, 30-, or 60-minute intervals, whichever you find easier. Jot down in a short note form that will be recognizable to you. There is no need to write out a lot of detail. Do this for one week and see where your time is going. At work, do the same. Keep it simple.*

I did this exercise shortly after setting up my consulting business. I thought I was working pretty hard and that I was focused on what I needed to do to win clients. I had been reaching out to people I knew to see if they needed help or could recommend me to others.

The exercise was very revealing. I was spending huge amounts of time (and money) having coffee and lunches with former colleagues and friends. Yes, some of them had the ability to hire me, but most did not. And many of them had the ability to recommend me, but not all, and I was spending up to three hours finding that out. For example, we would arrange to meet for lunch, which, including travel time from home, could take three hours out of my day. A simple 30-minute phone call from my home office was just as productive, especially with people who already knew me well.

It took a lot of discipline to turn down suggestions to meet in person from people whom I knew and liked, and instead suggest we have a quick call. However, the phone calls quickly clarified if I could help them or if they knew people who needed my help. Then I would set up meetings in person that were much more productive.

The exercise of tracking where your time goes might seem like a chore in itself, but much like keeping a food diary can reveal the fallacies of what you think you eat versus what you actually eat, this is a powerful tool to see where your day really goes.

Once you've done the exercise, you should see some obvious opportunities to make changes. The secret is then to schedule the things you really want to do, like going to the gym on your lunch break. Start by making it an appointment in your calendar that needs to be moved before it can be overridden. Now look at things that could be done by someone else.

We will come back to outsourcing and building a supportive infrastructure later in the book, but right now look at the amount of time spent on things that can be done by someone else. Take your time tracker and quickly highlight all of the tasks at home or work that can be delegated. For example, anyone can walk your dog, but only you can meditate. Anyone can fold laundry, but only you can take your shower or get your hair cut. Anyone can take notes at a meeting or set up the next meeting, but only you can attend parents' night at your child's school.

Start looking for opportunities to take things on your plate or in your inbox and move them out. Permanently.

I was once responsible for 30 direct reports, a ridiculous structure from an organizational point of view. Regardless, twice a year at performance review time I was responsible for writing 30 performance assessments, a task of many hours.

Instead, I had a performance conversation with each person, which was also required, and asked them at the end of it to write up their understanding of the conversation, their areas of development, and so on, and email it to me.

I would simply add that email to their performance file. If I didn't agree, or felt they missed something, I replied with those comments and put that email in the system. Suddenly an entire week had been cleared of tedious summations of assessments.

Take a look at how your time is being spent and see how you can pare away the extraneous in order to focus on the essentials, the things that help you, and the things you most enjoy.

2

Destination, Not Daydream

I n a nutshell: Clarify your ideal state. If you don't have a clear destination in mind, it's going to be hard to get there. Don't limit yourself by what you think is possible. In an ideal world, what would you be doing? Defining the ideal future and comparing it to the present brings into reality what needs to be changed and ignites the engine for forward motion.

In October 2016, I was speaking at a conference of corporate treasury professionals in Orlando. These individuals are the unsung heroes of the financial world, the people dedicated to the long-term financial health and sustainability of their companies. The businesses in which they work include all sectors of the economy, but they rarely make the headlines. They are long-term planners and think in three- to five-year funding cycles and often much longer.

Yet, when it came to planning their own careers, the topic on which I was speaking, they admitted they were much less diligent.

It's hard to achieve your goals if you don't have any.

That seems so obvious, yet the vast majority of the 500 people in the audience that day acknowledged they didn't have concrete goals for themselves despite a desire to realize change and progress in their lives.

You need to start by clarifying your ideal state. If you don't have a clear destination in mind, it's going to be hard to get there.

Sketch the Scene

Jo Peart, a native of Counties Dublin and Kildare in Ireland, had studied international marketing at college. It was a competitive course and many who applied were disappointed when they didn't receive a place in the program. The job prospects for graduates were considered good. After a year of studying in France as part of her degree, Jo was now also fluent in French. She began a career helping international companies expand into new markets, something she really enjoyed.

But around age 40, after a number of successful years in corporate life, she began thinking about the future and what kind of contribution she would be making with her life. She decided that she really wanted to be in medicine and wanted to retrain as a doctor.

"I did it because I had always remained interested in medicine, in particular the provision of health services and health policy. I hate talking about things rather than taking action, and I know from corporate life that the most effective cultural change is from within," Jo told me. She was surprised by the almost unanimous support from her friends and family and by the number of friends that had also considered going back and doing the same. It was those in medicine who questioned her decision to leave corporate life, where she was already earning substantially more than many of her peers, in order to be a student once more at the beginning of a daunting training program. Jo didn't see it that way at all.

"I did it because I could. I hadn't been pining; I enjoyed work always and as I had been lucky enough to grow in confidence. I was in a position to become somewhat successful and chose to follow a passion and a vision rather than a long-lost dream," she said.

She began medical school, and after completing residencies and internships—seven years after making the decision to retrain—she began working as a doctor. She now practices internal medicine at Connolly Hospital. She has never regretted the decision or regretted starting on a different path earlier.

"I was extremely fortunate to do the degree I did because of the friends it gave me and the career choice I made. I don't regret it at all. For a young person making a choice out of school, medicine is a very confining career; I'm glad I came to it after my other experiences," she said.

Jo's is an unusual case, but many of us spend years doing things we don't really enjoy because we think it would be impossible to change.

We worry we won't make as much money or will lose the security of our present situation. We think we might fail and, really, where we are is not so bad.

We rarely think we might be better off. We might be happier and actually earn more. We forget about the fact that change will come to our current situations. It won't remain static. Changes we can't foresee will make our current life less satisfying, and we become like the frog in increasingly warm water that doesn't notice the temperature is getting hotter until it's too late.

One way to avoid this is to write down your ideal future state. How would you like things to be in an ideal world? Assume no constraints for the moment. What would you ideally like to be doing? How would you be spending your time?

Most importantly, write it as though it was already real. Write it as though you are already in the future and you are describing your life.

Exercise: *Starting at the top of a clean page and write down your ideal future state. Pick a date in the future. Now write the qualities of how your life* *is at that future date. Use adjectives to describe how you feel, the texture of your life. What about the people who are most important to you? How are they? What are they doing?*

Don't limit yourself by what you think is possible. In an ideal world, what would you be doing? Writing it down and being ambitious about it is the first step to making it a reality.

Present-Day Reality

Now it's time to compare your ideal future state with your current reality. What does your current world look like? Be very factual and objective. Use short, concise sentences. Focus less on how you feel about current reality and more on the actual facts of your situation.

Exercise: *At the bottom of the same page, write your current reality. Note today's date. Where do you work, what's your marital status, do you have offspring, what is your financial situation, and so on?*

The idea here is to juxtapose your current state with your future state. By contrasting the two states, you create structural tension, and that tension gives you the impetus for action.

This is a technique pioneered by my good friend and great teacher Robert Fritz of Newfane, Vermont. If you're interested in learning more, I recommend his book *The Path of Least Resistance for Managers*.[1]

As Robert likes to say, reality is an acquired taste. But being more honest with yourself about your current reality is important, especially if you want to change it.

Now compare the two states: your current reality and your desired future state. Are they a million miles apart? Or are they not all that different? Maybe the desired future state seems unrealistic given current obligations and external realities.

For example, if your future ideal state is working less and spending more time with your family, you may look at your current reality and think it's not practical to quit your job or even cut back. You may also not be willing to change jobs to something less demanding that would mean a pay cut, so where does that leave you?

Don't give up. The most important thing is to be clear on the difference between the two states. The contrast is what helps you. You want to be really clear about your ideal life and where you are now. That allows you to see the differences and see what you could start changing right away.

I recommend practicing this technique with smaller things in order to become fluent in it. For example, take an important upcoming meeting, a presentation you have to give, or a trip you're going to take. You can also do it for dinner parties or projects at home. I always use it for planning Thanksgiving lunch, for example.

Here's the next step. After you have your ideal future state at the top of the page and current reality at the bottom, start filling in the middle of the page with tasks and things you need to do to move from one state to the other.

If you find it easier to practice this with something smaller than your life, do that.

You should have a column labeled "What" and one labeled "By When," in which you set a date for each task. The following is an example for an upcoming presentation.

Future State

It's November 15, I've just made a presentation to the board. I felt prepared and confident. I was clear about the points I wanted to make. The discussion was productive. They asked a lot of questions. They made some decisions and we agreed on next steps. They value my team's contribution and ideas. I feel happy that this is my job.

What—By When

Get input from team—November 5

Draft executive summary for distribution—
November 10
Draft talking points—November 12
Practice presentation—November 13

Current Reality

It's November 1, and I've just been asked to present to the board to seek approval for a project that will result in more resources for my team. My team is really keen to get going and is counting on me to get the project approved. I don't think all board members are on board. I need to sell the idea. I don't present to the board very often.

This may feel like a glorified to-do list at first, but there is something magical that happens when you juxtapose the reality you're in with the reality you desire. You will find that ideas arise out of things to do or people to talk to that wouldn't have come to mind by simply creating a list.

Defining the ideal future and comparing it to the present throws into relief what needs to be changed and ignites the engine for forward motion.

Leader Profile: Elizabeth Littlefield

Elizabeth Littlefield stepped down as the head of the Overseas Private Investment Corporation on January 20, 2017. OPIC is the U.S. government's development finance institution, charged with strengthening the private sector in developing countries and supporting U.S. companies to do business there.

In her seven-year tenure, she doubled the agency's portfolio to almost $22 billion, increased its focus on Africa, invested $1 billion annually on renewable energy, and worked with small American businesses in three-quarters of its projects—all at zero cost to U.S. taxpayers, because the agency is self-financing and, in fact, contributed $2.6 billion to the national deficit during her term. Not bad for someone who originally wanted to "write poetry or join the Peace Corps" and doesn't consider herself particularly good at banking.

She started her career at J.P. Morgan at the urging of her older brothers who thought she needed to start off with the imprimatur of a "blue chip" banking background, but then she worked her way into the lesser-known corners of the industry that connected to her passion for work with developing countries.

"I wasn't doing mainstream mergers and acquisitions and all this stuff you'd want to do to get ahead. I was trying to find a way I could do things like impact investing and emerging market stuff that was incredibly peripheral to J.P. Morgan's core business at the time. That was most appealing to me because I was really more interested in the people and progress in developing countries than I ever was in raw finance itself. I ended up convincing JPM to let me take the bank's first-ever sabbatical to go to West Africa for a year to set up microfinance institutions from scratch, applying my newly minted credit officer training skills to build access to finance for the poor."

A career at J.P. Morgan was followed by 10 years at CGAP, a global policy and research center promoting access to financial services for the poor, and then her appointment as CEO of OPIC in 2008.

Elizabeth wears her success lightly.

"I don't take myself super seriously, and I'm probably more frank and informal than some other leaders. More direct, more frank, more emotional, more personal. I hope that means I am authentic, for better or for worse."

That style extends to how she thinks about corporate culture.

"I don't like the external, public role as much as managing an organization to really make it hum, make it sing. I care deeply about the whole organism—being the best organization, with the happiest, most motivated, high-performing people in it, all working together in a way that's effective, tight, harmonious, positive, and focused on making the world a better place. I feel that there's something slightly maternal in that, and I really love it. It's an emotional and a personal, nurturing thing—to really care deeply about the organization and its people."

As for life outside of work, Elizabeth is married and the stepmother to two boys.

"Before I met Matt, I worked all the time and it was the driving force in my life. I think I drove my colleagues crazy. Then I met someone who had small children, and suddenly the whole axis of my world changed. I think I'm probably the only agency head in the entire U.S. government who doesn't really do work calls at night and doesn't do any work socializing at night. I go home and make dinner for the family and it's absolute. I probably do less networking and less professional socializing than almost anybody I know. Keeping that clean break hasn't really hurt me too much, I don't think."

Mind the Gap

"Mind the gap" is the famous message repeated daily over the public address system on the London Underground, the world's oldest underground train system. It warns commuters of the gap between the platform and the train into which they are stepping. It has inspired T-shirts, mugs, and other souvenirs for visitors to London.

It's a good metaphor for the gap between the reality in which we live and the future state to which we aspire. If we pay attention to the gap, it becomes much clearer what we need to change.

Sometimes the gap feels immense. When my son was very little, the gap between what I was doing and what I

wished I were doing yawned like a chasm. Although I had an interesting, well-paid job, it was very demanding and I often felt like I didn't want to work at all. I thought it would be lovely to press pause and simply take a couple of years off. I imagined picking my son up from nursery school every day and us hanging out together in the afternoons. At the time, his nanny got to do that while I went to work every morning and came back in time for dinner and bath time. But I didn't have the luxury of not working. I was a single parent. Even working part-time wouldn't have paid the bills we had.

As he grew older, my vision for what I most wanted to do changed. He was now in school all day and starting to get involved in afternoon sports. He wouldn't have been hanging out with me even if I had been free. I realized that what I wanted most was to work for myself. I wasn't sure how or what I would be doing, but I wanted to have my own business.

It took several more years and a change in my immigration status before I was finally able to hang out my shingle and set up my own consulting practice, but it was worth the wait. I didn't regret not doing it sooner. It hadn't been practical sooner. I had gained a huge amount of valuable experience in the interim and built up a powerful network of contacts. Now was the right moment to put that to work helping my clients.

It was hard work initially, and I made plenty of mistakes. Doing everything for the first time is exhausting, the first time. The second time, it gets easier. The third time, it's easier again and you know what to do. Then you start adding more new things and it's exhausting again, but you have a sense of momentum and you know where you're headed. You try to enjoy this phase of building the business and not be afflicted with the feeling that you will only be happy "when" you have more clients and "when" you have more incoming calls than outgoing ones.

Then, almost a year to the day I started my business, I got sick. I was diagnosed with ovarian cancer in February 2016. My world reeled. Just six weeks earlier, my sister Barbara, who is nine years younger, had been diagnosed with breast cancer in Dublin. Unbeknownst to us we were carriers of the BRCA1 gene, a gene mutation that causes an extremely high risk of breast and ovarian cancer in women.

We hadn't known about the gene and didn't have relatives with breast cancer. But it seemed it had traveled down on my father's side, concealed by the fact that he had no sisters, likely passed on from his mother who had died at home after an illness in the 1940s when he was very young. We now realized she had probably died of ovarian cancer.

I, on the other hand, was fortunate to be living in the 21st century in the United States and was treated quickly and expertly by some of the best doctors in this field. I am incredibly grateful for the care I received.

One of the many interesting things about facing my own mortality much sooner than anticipated was realizing that I was in fact living the life I wanted. I didn't regret having set up shop by myself. I didn't pine for the security of my salaried position and sick leave allowance. Being an entrepreneur was exactly what I wanted to be and being ill actually reinforced that fact.

I realized that if things didn't work out (a euphemism of some understatement), I would be happy knowing I had at least started doing that which I most wanted to do. I would have no regrets. That's the benefit of looking at the gap.

Go, No Go

Until one is committed, there is hesitancy, the chance to draw back, always ineffectiveness. Concerning all acts of initiative, there is one elementary truth, the ignorance of which kills countless ideas and splendid plans: that the moment one definitely commits oneself, then Providence moves too. All sorts of things occur to help one that would never otherwise have occurred. A whole stream of events issues from the decision, raising in one's favour all manner of unforeseen incidents and meetings and material assistance, which no man could have dreamt would have come his way. —W.H. Murray[2]

This quote is often misattributed to Goethe, the German poet and writer, but in fact William Hutchison Murray wrote it. Murray was a Welsh mountaineer and writer who served in the British army in North Africa during World War II. He was captured there by the Germans and narrowly escaped death by bonding with his captor over a shared love of mountain climbing. He survived three years in prisoner of war camps where he wrote the first draft of a book called *Mountaineering in Scotland* on toilet paper.

The quote is often misattributed to Goethe because Murray goes on to quotes lines from Goethe's play *Faust*: "Whatever you can do or dream you can, begin it. Boldness has genius, power and magic in it!"[3]

Many people who embark on new initiatives and ventures talk of the coincidences and chance encounters that then ensued, helping them toward their goals.

We tend not to think of Providence having a role in our daily lives yet we are familiar with the coincidence that happens when we come across something for the first time, a new word or phrase, for example, and then we start to see it in multiple places, despite never having seen it before.

The Providence Murray speaks of is propelled by action. The first step and the commitment to the endeavor set things in motion. Goethe urges us to "begin it" and that once begun, magic will be unleashed. Entrepreneurs and leaders often talk about the first step that launched their businesses or signified a turn in their careers.

I'm not talking about being reckless or foolhardy. There's no need to abandon your home and family to set off on that long-dreamed-of cross-country road trip. Nor am I suggesting you quit your job today to start your own business. (Although, if you don't have those commitments and want to do that, what are you waiting for?)

The purpose of getting clear on your future state and comparing it with your current reality is to make it clear what you could start doing today. You should be able to see some of the steps you could take that would bring you closer to your goal.

The very act of committing to the goal and beginning to move toward it starts to generate energy and other ideas. As you begin doing some of the smaller things on the list of actions you created, you will start to see other possibilities emerge.

Sometimes what emerges is the realization that this may not actually be what you want. As you move even closer to the goal and the reality of what it might mean, you may discover it's not really what you want or not as you imagined.

Crunching the numbers on financing a new project and mapping out the tasks needed to get there can have a sobering effect. Just as much as action and boldness bring about momentum toward a goal, they can also clarify that for right now, you're not ready to commit. But, if you are ready, there is no better time to start than now.

> *There is a tide in the affairs of men.*
> *Which, taken at the flood, leads on to fortune;*
> *Omitted, all the voyage of their life,*
> *Is bound in shallows and in miseries.*
> —William Shakespeare, *Julius Caesar*, Act IV

The Alternative Future

Dan Gilbert, a professor of psychology at Harvard University, has done some really interesting work on how we make choices and how we think about the future. His book *Stumbling on Happiness*[4] is a terrific read. In it, he uses science to show how terrible we are at imagining the needs of our future selves and what will make us happy.

Gilbert explores how we make decisions—everything from how we decide what to order at a restaurant to whom we should marry. He proves that we are as poor at predicting the future as we are at remembering the past. His most provocative recommendation is that we should not rely on our imagination to make decisions but rather on the use of surrogates. In other words, we should look at the experience of people who have done the thing we are thinking of doing in order to judge if it would work for us.

Gilbert also points out that we don't do that because we all believe our own situations are unique. In fact, we are not as special as we think we are and we can learn a lot from what has worked for others.

If that's the case, it makes sense for us to talk to people who have done the thing we most want to do.

My executive coaching clients invariably hold very senior roles in their companies. Among those looking to make a transition, the most successful are the ones who get lots of input on the transition. That doesn't mean they wander around telling everyone they meet about their plans or their desires to move on from their current roles. It means they do a lot of due diligence and research about the changes they want to make and take action to get information.

The following are six things they typically do, none of which involve telling the world they are looking for a change:

1. Map out the pros and cons of the current position, if the transition is voluntary.
2. List key influential people to ask for advice.
3. Draft a timeline with deadlines for doing research and making decisions.
4. List all of the factors, both external and internal, that they are aware of.
5. Schedule time in their calendar for research and meetings.
6. Identify who is doing the type of role they want and how they can get introduced to them.

My most successful clients are diligent about making time for this even though it can be very difficult when your current job is demanding and you have a full plate on the home front. If you can take even 15 minutes a day to work on this, you'll be amazed with the results.

Call this time "Future Me," and put it in your calendar as an appointment. Mark it as private if someone else sees your calendar. Pull out the previous six points and see how you can move them forward. Set a goal of reaching out to one person per week or month, whatever is realistic for you. Track your progress with a list of people you've met for informational interviews or advice. Did they have ideas of whom else you should meet? Have you called a headhunter? Spend your 15 minutes reviewing what you've accomplished and what's next on the list. If you're thinking of a move, have you scheduled a visit to see what it might be like to live there? Is there a way to try out a place or company without actually going there?

A coaching client of mine, Sonia, was the style editor at a major fashion magazine. She had been there for many years and had a great reputation, but the industry was changing rapidly. Revenues were shrinking across publishing, and social media celebrities attracting followers on Twitter and Instagram were upending the business model for fashion magazines. There had already been multiple rounds of layoffs. Sonia knew she needed to leave, but the rest of the industry seemed just as bad. She also knew that if she left voluntarily, she wouldn't be eligible for a redundancy package. She was the main breadwinner and had two kids in college, so packing up and figuring out what she would do later was not a viable option.

Instead, she decided to explore a partnership her company was involved in with a plus-size clothing designer. She had already been active on the project internally and decided to use it to learn more about the plus-size industry, which was rapidly expanding, to see if it might be a good fit for her.

Sonia was able to explore a new industry and build relationships with a market leader, all without leaving her current role. It gave her clarity about the industry being a place where her skills would be valued. She gained insight into the challenges faced by larger women in finding attractive clothes and found she had a passion for making that easier and more fun. That ultimately made the decision to leave the magazine an easy one and gave her a smooth transition to a new position.

What opportunities can you find to try out new roles or experiences you think you would enjoy? Who can you talk to about what their jobs are like? Dan Gilbert says surrogates are the most reliable ways of determining what will make us happy in the future. Find one or, like Sonia, be your own surrogate.

3

Inspiration vs. Perspiration

I n a nutshell: You need effort to get where you're going, but it doesn't have to be a slog. Effort trumps skill, but targeted effort combined with skill trumps everything. Slogging slows you down. Perfection will grind you into the ground. Be more creative and productive by giving your brain space to operate at its peak and taking care of the body in which it lies.

Our Brain as a Resource

Renowned psychotherapist Maryetta Andrews Sachs was musing to one of her patients about how much her field had changed in the 48 years since she had started practicing. Now in her 70s, Maryetta has worked in a community mental health clinic, private practice, and academia. One of the greatest shifts she noticed was the increased knowledge of how our brain works and its connection with the rest of our system.

"It used to be that we ignored the body, thinking it had no impact on the brain," said Maryetta. "But after practicing for decades, I am far more aware that most people seeking therapy have some type of trauma associated with their presenting problems and that attention to the mind–body link has to be made in order for treatment to be successful."

Our own brain is a resource in figuring out how we function and how to change behaviors that are unhelpful to us. If we can get better at understanding how we work, we can get better at changing the things we don't like.

There's plenty of research available, much of it in easily digestible forms, that helps us better understand the functioning of our own brains.

Check out TED Talks by people like Dan Gilbert, Martin Seligman, and others who are leaders in their fields in understanding what makes us tick and why we do the things we do. Most importantly, they offer us tools to help reprogram our brains a little to steer ourselves toward the outcomes we want and warn us against less helpful natural tendencies.

Daniel Kahneman offers some fascinating lessons in his book *Thinking Fast and Slow*.[1] Essentially his thesis is that there are some things we learn to do so well that they become intuitive and we do them with ease, using little effort or awareness. Other things are much harder for us and take great effort and energy. He creates two characters: "System 1" and "System 2" to represent fast and slow thinking, illustrating his point and making his book highly readable.

With practice, we can move some of our activities from slow thinking (System 2) to fast thinking (System 1). For example, when we first learn to drive a car, slow thinking is at work. We struggle to juggle all the things we must do at the same time: use foot pedals, check our rear-view mirrors, turn the wheel, and so on. Initially, it seems inconceivable that we could do all of this and also hold a conversation with someone or enjoy music on the radio. And yet, eventually the day comes when we are so proficient at driving that we have plenty of capacity left over to ponder what we should do on the weekend as we drive to work. That's fast thinking at work.

The same thing goes for many other tasks that initially daunt us, whether it's playing the piano or making a sales call. The more frequently we do it, the better we get at it and the less effort it takes.

Kahneman also has warnings for what happens when we over-rely on fast thinking and aren't even aware that we are making decisions or that we are doing them based on very little information. We translate anecdotes as data and make assumptions we don't test. This trips us up when we think we know more than we do.

Here's why Kahneman's work matters for us. If you are trying something new, you will generally find it is harder to do and takes more out of you than doing something at which you are proficient.

Take the case of Melanie, a coaching client of mine at a global consumer products company. Melanie took up a new role at headquarters, joining from a subsidiary of the parent company. She was recognized as a high-flyer and considered an internal hire. She knew a number of people at headquarters already and was inheriting a team that needed to be restructured and turned around. The move also involved a change of city and leaving her social network in Chicago.

When we first spoke, she said she was finding it very difficult not to be as confident in what she was doing as she had been in her old job and that people were expecting her to immediately perform with the same productivity as before. She was also feeling exhausted after days of getting less done than she was used to.

When we applied Kahneman's thinking to her case, the cause was apparent. She was using System 2, slow thinking, by necessity because so much of what she was doing was new and unfamiliar. It was going to take some time to get to the level of efficiency of brain function that she had been used to in her old job where System 1, fast thinking, was in charge. That was also why she was so tired. Slow thinking uses more fuel than fast thinking.

Melanie realized she needed to give herself a break for not being instantly as productive and efficient as she had been before and also to push back on people expecting the same immediate performance from her.

Understanding what was happening in her brain made that much easier to do.

Effort Trumps Skill

In his book *Outliers*,[2] Malcolm Gladwell popularized the notion that practicing 10,000 hours was the secret of success in a diverse range of fields from music to software to the law. However, to most of us mere mortals, reading tales of what Bill Gates, The Beatles, and Mozart had in common, although interesting, is not that helpful. Most of us are not phenoms, whom if given the right circumstances of birth and hours of undisturbed practice from an early age will go on to achieve greatness.

However, what Gladwell did get right for the rest of us was the importance of practice. It does not need to be 10,000 hours, which seems so extraordinarily unrealistic, but practice is in fact the secret to success in most fields. Luck and timing also help, but here we are focused on the things over which we have some control.

Angela Duckworth, a student of Martin Seligman, who was mentioned earlier in the book, is a pioneer in the field of "grit." She has studied the role perseverance plays in acquiring skill and being successful at a given endeavor. Her book *Grit: The Power of Passion and Perseverance*[3] is a useful read for anyone convinced that fate and family determine the path of one's life.

Duckworth posits that grit, the ability to persevere despite setbacks and obstacles, is the true predictor of success in life. She has a grit test that one can take to check one's own level of grit. I scored poorly the first time I took it, but I intend to persevere and raise my score!

Her conclusion after reviewing masses of data and conducting hundreds of interviews with athletes, musicians, teachers, and others is that there is a formula to success and it looks like this: talent x effort = skill; skill x effort = achievement.

Duckworth found that the swimmers who were most successful had consistently trained harder and the students who did better had worked harder, even when they initially started as less talented or gifted than their peers. In other words, effort was a more important predictor of outcome than apparent talent.

Duckworth's work builds on that of Carol Dweck, who talks about "growth mindset," which is the belief that effort and application result in improvement, or "I can't do that yet."[4]She compares that to a "fixed mindset," which is the belief that if it doesn't come naturally, it doesn't come at all, or "I am someone who can't do that."

The wonderful news from our point of view of all this research is that effort is far more important than natural ability. If you simply make more of an effort, you stand to improve.

Here's the important caveat: The effort must be focused.

I was wondering why I never get faster at running. I have been running for about eight years. I run a steady 10-minute mile pace, occasionally nine minutes, and I can generally do four to eight miles at a time, but not further.

Then I compare myself with my son, whom I used to easily outrun when he was 11 or 12 years old. He is now 15 years old and runs a five and half minute mile pace in cross-country races.

The answer isn't simply that he's younger and has gotten stronger. He practices with his school team six days a week. There is a plan for their practice and it varies. The runners are timed and have goals for each session in terms of speed and distance. Then they compete against others and see how they have improved.

Meanwhile, I do the exact same four- or eight-mile loop in my local park two or three times a week at the exact same pace. Of course I am not improving! Duckworth had the same realization in her book.

It takes focused effort to improve, but it can be done. So if you think you can't get to the next level professionally or achieve a dream in a personal hobby, reflect on how much real effort you are putting into that goal. How much are you blaming circumstances and others for your inability to achieve what you want?

If it's mostly about the effort, that's really good news and life should look a whole lot better right now.

The Curse of Perfection

Seeking perfection can be very debilitating for the following reasons:

1. **Your focus on detail can leave you missing the big picture.** As you format and reformat a document, you fail to notice new information that will impact the overall argument you're making.

2. **You fear failure and are often hesitant to act in case you won't be right.** This can be as simple as not wanting to ask a "stupid" question in a meeting or failing to seize a professional opportunity for fear you won't do it well enough.

3. **It's exhausting.** The problem with perfection is that it's in the eye of the beholder. You can work and re-work something forever. There is usually little meaningful benefit from doing so. At best, it's incremental improvement. Sometimes you have even made matters worse.

4. **It's really hard on the people around you.** If only you can do things "the right way," you create disincentives for others to try or leave them believing they will never be able to do it for themselves. This happens as often at home as it does at work.

Ask yourself the following questions and answer "yes," "no," or "sometimes":

1. Do you have high expectations of yourself?
2. Do you often criticize yourself for not achieving what you set out to do?
3. Does it matter very much to be right?
4. Do you get very irritated at things not being as they should?
5. Do you like to explain things in detail?

Now tally your scores; yes = 1, no = 0, and sometimes equals 0.5.

If you scored between 2.5 and 5.0, you may suffer from the curse of perfection.

If you scored lower, keep reading, because someone you know almost certainly has this affliction and learning how it impacts them could be helpful to them and to you.

"The perfect is the enemy of the good" is a phrase that exists in multiple languages and has its origins from the 1600s. Voltaire quotes it in his *Philosophical Dictionary*[5] in 1764, "Le mieux est l'ennemi du bien"—more accurately translated as "The better is the enemy of the good."

Winston Churchill had a related saying: "Perfect is the enemy of progress."[6]

Robert Watson Watt, who developed radar in Britain during the World War II, had an entire philosophy on this concept. He termed it "the cult of the imperfect," and described it as, "Give them the third best to go on with; the second best comes too late, the best never comes."[7]

Ultimately, that is the problem with perfection for us; the timing is never perfect, we never have enough information, and things will almost certainly change. The challenge is to press on and take some risk in allowing things not to be perfect.

Many couples wrestle with whether the time is right to have their first child. The changes to their lifestyles, income, and own bodies seem immense and daunting. You would suppose that should be doubled when it comes to contemplating a second child, but it rarely is. Having done something once, doing it again feels much less daunting.

The same is true for changes you want to make in your own life. If you can press on, initially making minor changes and moving your way forward toward your goal, you will find your fear of not being perfect, and things not being perfect around you, will diminish.

Exercise: *What are the things you hesitate to do because you don't think you would do them well? Perhaps you duck away from public speaking, never* *raise your hand to volunteer, or do not entertain friends as often as you'd like.*

List the things you steer clear of, things that have the ability to benefit you or bring you pleasure. Now pick one from the list and plan to do it within the next seven days. Start small. Maybe its presenting to your own team, asking someone to mentor you, or speaking up at a town hall. Make yourself do it and see what happens. Then pick the next thing on the list. It will get easier as you work your way down the list.

Friluftsliv

If it is true that psychotherapy never really paid much attention to the brain as a physical organ, it paid even less attention to the rest of the body and the importance it plays in our well-being and happiness.

Ever more research is uncovering the benefits of exercise to our mental state, moods, brain functioning, and ability to fight disease. It's now said that if exercise were a pill, it would be prescribed more widely than aspirin.

In April 2015, the Academy of Medical Colleges released a report citing the benefits of exercise as a "miracle cure"[8] and huge meta-analysis of numerous longitudinal studies have demonstrated the long-term benefits of exercise.

In the ancient world, the Roman poet Juvenal coined the term "Mens sana in corpore sano," which has been translated as "a healthy mind in a healthy body."[9] The

Romans believed that the foundation for the good life involved both the physical and mental.

Most of us might acknowledge the benefits of exercise, but we find it hard to actually apply and make time for it. Our lives are already busy and adding another "should do" seems unrealistic. We are often good at intellectualizing and resolving to do better—just witness the flood of health club applications in January each year. By March, the flood of new people has receded and the regulars have the place to themselves again.

If you really want to reap the benefits of exercise you have to build it into your life and make it a routine, not something you have to think about. If you are making a decision each time about whether to go for a run or get to the gym, you are relying on will power, which is notoriously overrated.

Building exercise into your day offers you the best chance of success. Keeping your expectations low also helps. So, for example, don't sign up right away for a triathlon; just make sure you have a routine that has you running three times a week, or getting to the gym on Tuesdays and Thursdays at the same time. If you have friends who are also interested, coopt them. That improves your chances of going as you now have a commitment to keep.

My friend Caroline walks briskly for an hour every morning with some of her neighbors. She says she would never dream of rolling out of bed on a winter morning to do that by herself, but the fact that it's already planned and they are expecting her takes away the desire to find excuses or cancel. They chat as they walk and the time goes quickly.

Another friend, Mark, hates the gym, but he loves food and fine wine. He knows he can't enjoy eating and drinking at the rate he does and feel well if he doesn't exercise. He schedules his personal trainer in the mornings and gets it out of the way so he can get on with the things he really enjoys.

Being outdoors and in nature when you exercise offers additional benefits. The Nordics call it *friluftsliv*, literally

translated as "open air living." It means enjoying life out of doors and spending time in nature.

A walk in the woods or countryside beats a walk on a treadmill (although the treadmill beats no walk at all, so I won't knock it too much). Getting outdoors to exercise has a restorative effect on the mind in addition to getting you those endorphins.

Easier in summer but especially important in winter, a shot of *friluftsliv* can inoculate us from the winter blues.

The most important aspect of exercise is that it should be part of our routine and that it be vigorous. Strolls don't count. You don't get the benefit of endorphins with a stroll.

Endorphins are the chemicals released when you exercise. They interact with receptors in your brain that reduce your perception of pain. They also trigger a positive feeling in the body similar to morphine. They can create a feeling of euphoria, sometimes described as a "runner's high"—that high also impacts your outlook on life.

In short, exercise benefits your mind as much as your body. It reduces stress and anxiety, can boost your self-esteem, and wards off depression. It allows you to sleep better, which sets you up for a better day and ultimately a better life. Treat it with the importance it deserves and you'll start to reap the rewards.

Leader Profile: Lars Thunell

Lars Thunell is an ideal example of someone who has created the type of portfolio life discussed in Chapter 9. He retired as CEO of IFC, the private sector arm of the World Bank, where he tripled investment to $20 billion annually and doubled the proportion of that investment to companies operating in the world's poorest countries. Prior to that he had been CEO of SEB, a leading Swedish bank, where the successor he helped choose, Annika Falkengren, an outlier as a female bank CEO, is still at the helm.

In response to the question of how he was so successful professionally, he says:

"That's a hard question to answer about yourself. I had the good fortune to get a good education, and to have a terrific wife, Yvonne, a partner. Together we made a great team. And I worked pretty hard on things. Also, being in the right place at the right time and having luck in that sense. Luck always helps. So does a crisis."

A crisis and luck can be equally helpful?

"I've been involved in quite a few crises. Crises are not always bad things. They create opportunity. If you can take that opportunity when it's there and not be scared, you can do things."

During the Swedish banking crisis in the 1990s, Lars was tapped to lead Securum, a "bad bank" holding toxic assets, which ultimately made money for the country. That experience served him well during the global financial crisis that began in 2008, when he was at the helm at IFC.

"If you can think clearly and try to define your way out of a crisis with a constructive solution, opportunities will come up. Opportunities always come after a crisis. The world looks different afterward. It's in everything, even a crisis with a friend or partner, that's an opportunity to move forward. In relationships, either things go downhill completely or it's an opportunity to go to the next level."

Of the things that make up a rich life—job, family, hobbies, friends, and so on, Lars believes you have to find points of overlap. You can't try to do everything.

"I don't think you can have a terrific career, good family life, be out a lot with friends socializing, do extreme sports, and so on. You have to figure out how they overlap. If you're interested in skiing or sailing, you do it with your family. Then it overlaps. Yvonne and I share a lot of common interests, so we can be together when we do our hobbies and sports."

"You need to prioritize, like everything in life. There is always another thing you can do, so you have to be disciplined. In the office you have to learn how to get good people on your team, to delegate and then you have to trust them. It comes back to your personality; some people find that hard. It's a matter of trust. You have to trust the people. It's just like in an orchestra or a sailing crew. If you're the conductor, you'll never play the violin as well as the lead violinist. So don't try to."

In his portfolio career, post-corporate life, Lars serves on a number of boards and as chairman of the board of ARC Insurance Company Limited and Access Health International. He does a lot of work with smaller companies and entrepreneurs in the electricity, energy efficiency, and sustainability sectors.

"I got good advice when I retired, which was that you don't need to take on many things. Your life will be full. And if you've been successful, you don't need external validation, so you can choose to do things that are fun."

"I have three simple criteria now for anything I do professionally. Will it be fun? Will it do good? Is it remunerative? Because people value more of which they pay for. So when I look from that perspective, even if it's prestigious or well paid, I won't do it if I don't think it will be fun," he says smiling broadly.

Meditate Away

If we think of the mind as a physical organ that needs tending, one of the most effective ways of doing that is through meditation. Meditation or mindfulness is essentially the art of training the mind in awareness. It's a skill that allows us to separate a little from the emotions and distraction we experience. If we can observe the emotions and identify them, we are already slightly apart from them. The act of noticing what we are feeling is only possible if we have stepped back a little and are looking at the emotion.

That simple step of observing what we are feeling creates some space in the mind and reduces the strength of the emotion. If we are not wrapped up in the emotion but are watching it instead, we have a little distance and that changes how we relate to the emotion.

Easier said than done, you say. What about when we are roiled by really strong emotions and are losing our cool? It's rather difficult to step back and think "Oh, there I go, I'm furious because that person has cut me off in traffic and I'm already late."

That's where training the mind comes in. Meditation or mindfulness is simply the skill of training the mind to be aware of what's happening. Being able to notice the ebb and flow of emotions and label them is enormously helpful in creating stability in the mind. That stability in turn contributes to feelings of calm and gives us the confidence to tolerate changing situations and our own emotions.

We soon discover that the mind is a little like Irish weather. If you don't like what's happening right now, wait a while and it will change.

It helps to know that good and bad feelings come and go, and that holding tightly on to them or chasing them away won't help. The act of noticing them gives us confidence that they will change, whether we want them to or not.

Research on the benefits of meditation has increased dramatically as our understanding of how the brain works has increased.

Srinivasan Pillay, whom I met several years ago on a course for high-potential staff at the World Bank, has done intriguing research at Harvard Medical School on the brain and impact of meditation. A physician who combines scientific research with the study of human potential, he has demonstrated the benefits from the perspective of neuroscience.[10]

In the past, research into the benefits of meditation was usually focused on small groups, including communities of Buddhist monks living lives of quiet contemplation. Demonstrating that their stress levels were lower than the rest of us was hardly compelling evidence of the benefits of meditation. It was also not a useful solution to people seeking more calm in their lives. Taking off to a Tibetan retreat or spending several hours a day meditating is not a practical option for most of us.

Then larger-scale and longitudinal studies became more common, such as the one undertaken by the Health and Human Performance Laboratory at Carnegie Mellon University, recently published in the *Journal of Biological Psychiatry*.[11]

These studies demonstrate that the benefits of meditation include reduced stress and reduced risk for various diseases and better sleep quality. Brain scans of participants showed differences in those who underwent mindfulness meditation. There was more activity, or communication, among the portions of their brains that process stress-related reactions and other areas related to focus and calm. Four months later, those who had practiced mindfulness showed much lower levels in their blood of a marker of unhealthy inflammation than the relaxation group, even though few were still meditating.[12]

When I spent a few days at Kripalu, a yoga retreat in the Berkshire Mountains of Massachusetts, I joined a meditation class during which someone asked what kind of meditation is the best. The answer was, "The kind you do."

The secret to unlocking the benefits of meditation is a regular daily practice. It doesn't really matter which guru or app or school of mindfulness. What matters is that it is habitual and that you are building stability of awareness that you can use through the day.

My personal favorite is Andy Puddicombe, the creator of Headspace.[13] He has a website, an app for your smartphone, and a selection of guided and unguided meditation programs to choose from. There are some great cartoons to help you understand some of the principles. And he's not trying to sell you anything. There is no merchandise to buy. He is simply trying to help you train your mind and achieve greater calm and contentment in your life.

Combine this with exercise and you'll be on your way to a healthy mind in a healthy body, and you will be well prepared to enjoy the things most important to you.

4

Investing in Infrastructure

n a nutshell: Investing in yourself and building systems that support you is key to being successful in changing your life. When it comes to behaving differently, willpower is highly overrated. Beating yourself up endlessly is equally unproductive. You need to build habits that will help you get where you want to go and invest now to optimize performance. This is often more important at home than at work.

Take Away Willpower

"You'll see I wear only gray or blue suits," former President Barack Obama said. "I'm trying to pare down decisions. I don't want to make decisions about what I'm eating or wearing. Because I have too many other decisions to make."

Former President Obama was speaking to writer Michael Lewis early in his tenure for an article in *Vanity Fair* magazine. Obama had realized a critical component to having a productive day: reduce decision-making.

Reducing decision-making at its heart is about creating routines. In this case, the routine is to always pick from a half a dozen nearly identical suits and then move on to the more important parts of the day.

Routine has been shown to be an incredibly powerful way of creating new habits and new behaviors. Research now shows that routine is the secret weapon behind many successful behavior change programs including Alcoholics Anonymous and Weight Watchers.[1]

Why is creating a routine so powerful? Simply put, because willpower is incredibly overrated. Willpower

requires much more energy, thought, decision-making, and calculations of cost-benefit at the very moment when we are least capable of thinking longer term.

For instance, when faced with the choice at the end of the day at home between collapsing on the couch with your iPad versus changing your clothes and heading back out to the gym, you can bet the couch is a more attractive offer. However, if you've built a gym visit into your day, on the way in to work, over lunch, or at the end of the day, you are much more likely to get there.

We are creatures of habit and the more habitual we make the behaviors we want to see, the easier we make it for ourselves.

"I knew when I was in my 20s that I would not want to be taking up exercise in my 50s only to discover how hard that would be," says Bruce McNamer, CEO of the Greater Washington Community Foundation. "I'd seen older colleagues be forced to take up new exercise regimens because of health issues and struggle to get to optimal fitness. So, I decided early to build running into my daily routine. Now I run four miles or so every morning, whether I like it or not. Whenever I travel, I throw a pair of shoes and shorts into my bag. I don't even think about it anymore. It's simply part of my life, like brushing my teeth."

It's not just exercise that lends itself to routine. Everything we do or want to do that requires repetition to improve or streamline, lends itself to routine.

A senior Australian diplomat I know always orders fish or seafood whenever she eats out. She simply scans the menu for the fish or shellfish dishes and picks the healthiest one. Almost every menu has something involving fish. She rarely cooks fish at home but because she eats out frequently, she can ensure she is eating a regular amount of low-fat protein to balance the red meat she prepares at home for her family. She simply doesn't look at the rest of the menu anymore because the habit is so ingrained.

The trick in introducing new habits is to make it as easy as possible to succeed and to persevere for three weeks. Research has shown that doing anything regularly for 21 days consecutively can turn into a habit.[2] And habits, as we know, are hard to break.

Leader Profile: Bruce McNamer

Bruce McNamer is CEO of the Greater Washington Community Foundation, a public charity that acts as a hub for philanthropy in the greater Washington, D.C., region. Most cities have a community foundation. They work by both accepting donations and making grants, and by partnering with businesses, donors, local government, and nonprofits to improve the communities they serve. He was previously CEO of Technoserve, a global nonprofit that helps farmers and cooperatives in developing countries increase the value of their agricultural produce and access new markets.

Bruce is disarmingly frank in talking about having had a charmed life that started with where he was born in Billings, Montana, and to whom, as the eldest of five siblings.

"I've been very blessed. So much of life's success is just the accident of our birth, our parents, where we are born. The starting point is so much. My parents were very committed to family life. They instilled in us the value of delayed gratification, of public service, hard work, and a religious faith. We read together as a family. We were encouraged and expected to do well," Bruce recalls.

"So I developed an ability to work hard and focus, and I had a certain amount of ambition. Those have all stood me in good stead. Then I was continually blessed. I went to a good school, Harvard, which then in turn led to successive equally pedigreed institutions," he said.

Bruce attended Stanford Law and Business schools, was a White House Fellow, and worked for McKinsey and later J.P. Morgan.

"It keeps compounding. You move from a great school to a good company and so on. The people hiring you figure the others before them must know something. And it goes on; once you've been a CEO one place, you can be a CEO another place," he says frankly, noting the inherent unfairness for those who don't start from the same spot. He is also aware of what you need to do when you get these opportunities.

"I was always an avid participant in whatever I did. I was curious, disciplined, and open to wonder and adventure and trying things. My ambition was to have a full and rich life. And I had always aspired to leadership roles and that has built on itself; from high school to college to companies."

But it hasn't been a completely linear trajectory of success.

"I worked at three failed startups. It felt bad. It was scary and I worried about whether there was something out there for me. I was depressed for a while," he admits.

What does he think has been most important to his success in running various-sized organizations?

"Business school doesn't prepare you for management. What you need to know is how to run a good process, how to have a hard conversation with an employee, how to manage a budget, how to run good meetings. Things like that, that you learn on the job," he says.

The other critical skills he believes include the value of process, of good governance, early attention to risk in an organization, and the importance of good people.

"I want to like and respect the people I work with. I don't want to work with jerks. I don't care how talented they are. I've seen how toxic that can be. And beyond those considerations, the old adage of 'slow to hire, quick to fire' makes a lot of sense to me," he explains.

Bruce believes in deliberately creating a corporate culture that simultaneously expects high competence and accountability, but also kindness and respect.

"Kind is really important. We spend so much time at work. It's important. I want a culture where people are accountable and competent of course, but also where people are kind and respectful," he says.

In terms of personal productivity, Bruce believes in the power of lists, the calendar, and discipline, discipline, discipline.

"I am the world's worst multitasker. I set a watch and say to myself, I've got 20 minutes to do this, or 45 minutes when I will only focus on this one thing. Then I'll give myself three minutes to check my email and then on to the next task," he explains.

"I believe in the power of a calendar, both for day-to-day as well annual. You need to organize the organization around that. Every week I step back and take a look at the big picture for 15 minutes. What are the big things that have to happen, sooner or later, or the niggling concern I keep putting off? What are the things that would propel the organization forward or what do I need to be thinking about the board? I write it down, and then get back in," he adds.

Bruce is single and doesn't have children, and he recognizes there are some advantages inherent to that.

"I work hard but I don't work killer hard. I have not had to make the trade-offs that people who have families have to. That's a very real thing. I have plenty of opportunities to relax with friends, have a social life, and to exercise regularly—that's really important to me and I learned that early," he acknowledges.

"I think I've always been aware of the trap of not paying attention to life. I will step back periodically and ask myself how life is going, to be clear on my mission, vision, and values. So when I'm 75 years old I can look back and be proud of what I've done. Then I ask myself, what am I doing toward that end this year?"

"I'm aware of making choices to have a fuller life, like choosing to go to the Peace Corps and putting off graduate school. It wasn't an obvious choice to my peers. But I thought it would be a great experience and it was."

"I'm a generally happy person, and at this point in my life I realize that will likely always be the case. That takes a lot of the pressure off. I'm grateful for the life I have had. I've had the freedom and opportunity to shape it because of where I came from, where I was born. I have been very fortunate," he concludes.

ROI at Home

I was working with a professional women's network at a large financial institution when Lorena raised her hand. The topic of the discussion was career management and ways to progress more rapidly within the organization. She was a mid-level manager in her 30s working in infrastructure financing in Latin America. She wanted to know when it would get easier. Lorena had two small children, a husband who also worked full time, and she needed to travel for her job.

"I feel like I am running to stand still and although I am doing well professionally, I can barely manage to save anything. Will it always be like this?" she asked.

Many other women in the room nodded. It's a common theme, and not just for women.

Hugh was a senior treasury professional at an international bank. He had lived in Norway, his wife's home country, and had gotten used to the idea that they would partner equally at home and he would have as much time to enjoy their children as she did. He was finding life more difficult in the United States without state-funded preschools and an assumption that the working day ended around 7 p.m., not 5 p.m. as it had for him in Norway.

There isn't an easy answer to structural issues like lack of parental leave or affordable day care. These need to be tackled at a government level, so make sure your elected representative knows these issues matter to you and vote accordingly. We can't all move to Norway.

In the meantime, here's a chart worth bearing in mind.

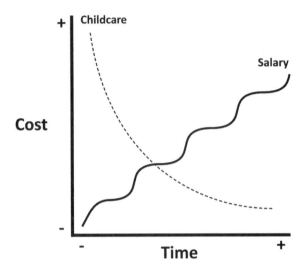

The important thing to realize is that if you have children, *the associated costs tend to be higher earlier in your career when your earning is not at its peak.* Later, as you progress in your career you'll be earning more and your child-related costs will start to level out.

Think about it: When you have one or two preschool-age children, you may need to pay for a babysitter in addition to preschool or Montessori tuition. The preschool day is so short, you need someone to take care of them for the rest of the day while you're at work. If they are in an all-day day care, you might be paying up to $2,000 a month for two children.

But when those children start school, your costs start to decline. You no longer need a full-time sitter and won't be paying for preschool. You may still need a babysitter, but only for a couple of hours in the afternoon or the children may attend free afterschool programs. Meanwhile, your salary will have increased as you progress at work.

The point to think about here is how investing in your career and your mental health will increase your longer-term earning power. As your earnings increase over time, you'll be able to look further ahead and save more for college, the next crunch period.

That means outsourcing as much as you can and paying more than you want to for good child care and help at home. The near-term return is being less stressed and harried, allowing you to be happier at home and more productive at work, giving you the bandwidth over time to take on more senior roles and new assignments, with higher pay.

Make a list of the chores you currently do that someone else could do just as well. That list will be different for everyone but could include paying someone to clean the house, do laundry, walk the dog, and pick up the children early so you aren't all stuck in rush hour traffic. Treat yourself by occasionally sending out laundry. There are now apps for "wash and fold" laundry services with free pick-up and drop-off. Try a meal prep service like Blue Apron to streamline dinnertime and reduce last-minute shopping. Order groceries online and have them delivered. Or pay your sitter a little extra to fix supper dishes that are ready when you come home.

Invest similarly in your relationship, if you're in one. A regular date night and some adult time provide a much-needed break in your week and the reconnection time that you both need. Heading out for dinner and a movie or game night with friends does the same. That's an investment that will also pay off longer term and may keep you away from the divorce courts.

Focus on the things that you alone want to do, like kids' bath time or story time, and invest in reducing the things that anyone could do. It's an investment that your present self will enjoy, while your future self will just assume was a smart move.

These tips don't only apply to parents of young children. For anyone who has commitments beyond work that include chores you don't enjoy, think about whether you would be better off having someone else do them and enjoying that discretionary time instead. Instead of cleaning your apartment on Saturday morning, go to an exercise class, catch up with a friend, or visit a museum and come home to a clean apartment.

The return on investment is clear: If you give yourself a break on the home front, you'll be better able to do well at work and increase your earning potential. Spend what you can now knowing things will get easier over the long haul.

Exercise: List out all the tasks you do at home or outside work. This may be a very long list. Don't despair! Do this quickly to get a sense of where your time and energy is going.

Add four columns to the right of the task list with the following headers:

1. *I enjoy (yes or no)*
2. *Takes longer than 30 minutes (if yes, how long)*
3. *Could be done by someone else (yes or no)*
4. *Cost to have someone else do (estimated $ amount)*

Now take stock. Go for low-hanging fruit. If there are things you dislike, that chunk of time could be occupied by someone else for a reasonable amount (for example, washing the car or mowing a large lawn). Consider paying someone to do that. If, on the other hand, you enjoy that task and it's something you do with other family members (picturing small children with garden hose and soapy car), then leave as is and look for other opportunities.

Invest Professionally

Marshall Goldsmith, one of the most famous executive coaches in the world, is always surprised when other coaches say their clients are confidential.

"I don't understand that at all. All of my clients are happy to say I have coached them. It's a badge of honor. It means they are smart and have invested in themselves," Marshall told a group of coaches and consultants at a conference in Las Vegas in March 2016.

It has become more common for senior executives to talk openly about having a coach. Many think it shows self-awareness and openness to learning. It has become cool to admit you don't know everything.

For executives below the C-suite, having a coach is an indication of the company's belief in your potential and value. Why else would they invest in a coach for you? You're obviously going somewhere if they are spending money on you.

Poor performers tend not to receive coaching. They may get some counseling if they are on a performance improvement plan. Some large companies will offer employees who are being let go the services of a coach, but that's usually someone to help you draft your resume and prepare for interviews.

If there is coaching available at your company, take advantage of it. Even an average coach can be helpful. You'll be surprised what comes up when you have to articulate your goals for your life and career. You'll also benefit from reflecting on issues that bother you at work.

One coaching client I worked with couldn't understand why she kept getting so upset about things that were happening at work. She was losing sleep because of being asked to focus more on things she didn't think were important, like preparing the meetings of the senior team, while she was told to cut back on spending time with new associates who were keen to connect with each other and find community.

After a simple coaching exercise to uncover her core values, it became apparent that her values weren't in line with the team she was on. She valued community and family very highly and was driven to be very efficient; hence, she found preparing for meetings very unsatisfying. This realization led her to rethink her entire career at the firm and decide she really wanted to be a solo consultant with an arms-length relationship and the freedom to work for others.

Taking advantage of coaching is one way of investing in yourself. The other is to get on a program for high potentials. In larger organizations, these are formal processes often involving nominations to programs. Find out what is done at your organization. Your boss may not know, but human resources should be aware. You want to find out the requirements and time frame and get yourself nominated.

If there is no high-potential program at your company, see if there's a formal mentoring program and, if there isn't, suggest you start one. There is no reason why you can't help create a mentoring program. You just need the support of one senior person to get started. The advantage of setting up a formal program is that you'll get the credit for taking the initiative and you'll be able to network with peers and rotate mentors over time.

Failing that, seek out a mentor and ask them to commit to meeting once a month for 30 to 60 minutes. You'll be surprised at how willing senior people are to doing this. First off, it's flattering. Second, mentors always gain insight and intelligence from what's going on at other levels in the company, which can be very valuable when interacting with their peers.

Whatever you end up doing, make sure you optimize it and get the most out of it.

Case Study: Mazen was based in the Middle East for a global financial services firm. He had been selected to be part of a high-potential cohort that would be meeting twice a year and receiving leadership training, including how to be more influential and effective in the organization. Mazen's boss thought very highly of him and wanted to help him progress in his career. One reservation he expressed was that Mazen often didn't contribute much at regional team meetings or to corporate projects. He didn't speak up or take the lead on issues. Mazen said the reason was that he was too busy and was focused on delivering his program.

Although he was on the high-potential program, the pattern repeated itself. Mazen was often outside the room, taking calls and answering emails for the business back home and missing out on the program and networking opportunities with colleagues and program sponsors. Who misses out in a case like this? Arguably both Mazen and his boss do. Mazen fails to develop and is less likely to be offered greater responsibility, and his boss doesn't get to tap a great resource.

Prudence and Abundance

It may seem unwise to spend money on making your life easier on the assumption of higher future earnings. It's easy for others to suggest you "invest" in a date night or home cleaning service. They are not looking at a declining bank balance trying to justify the cost of a sitter and reconcile your current anxiety about finances with your future happiness.

I am a big believer in being prudent while thinking abundantly. It's easier to think abundantly if you have a good understanding of your finances. That starts with understanding your current financial situation.

Take a look at what you are spending your money on. Track it using a simple notebook and pen or get an app that will keep track for you. Do this for a month or two and take a look at the patterns. Separate out your fixed costs (mortgage or rent) and your quasi-fixed costs (utilities or insurance). Now see if you can reduce any of those. Is it a good time to refinance your mortgage? Can you reduce any utility costs through energy efficiency? Set up your utilities to be paid automatically and sign up for "budget plans" that smooth out payments and allow you to pay the same amount every month on utilities that fluctuate seasonally.

Check whether your insurance policies give you the coverage you need. You may be able to reduce your car insurance if you've got an older car and you're willing to self-insure for damage to your car when you're at fault.

Make a plan to clear any credit card debt. You might want to consolidate it or take out a home equity loan that will have lower interest in order to clear the debt faster.

Then take a look at your spending habits. Can you reduce your grocery bill or takeout habit? Try setting a budget for entertaining and sticking to it. Your friends are glad to gather at your place whether you serve simple roast chicken or expensive rack of lamb. Suggest less expensive places to meet when you go out.

What are you spending on clothes, at Starbucks, or on lousy meals at your company's cafeteria? Once you have a sense of where the money is going, you can see where you can make changes and decide what is really important to you. If you really like your high-end gym, maybe you can trade off by bringing lunch in to work and saving on lunch costs.

You need to cover the basics like insurance, retirement, health care, and savings. You need a rainy day fund for large unexpected expenses. Set those all up to be automatically deducted so you don't see them and you live on the rest. That's called "paying yourself first." Then comes everything else, like your favorite takeout place.

Once you feel you have some control of your current finances, you're better placed to live abundantly. That doesn't necessarily mean living large, but it means being clear about what is important to you and being conscious about where you're spending your money.

If you want to spend time visiting with family, make sure it's a real vacation. If it's not, keep the trips short and realize not everyone has to go. Shorter is often better. A weekend in a nice inn may restore you more than a week in a second-rate hotel.

Look for ways to have fun that don't cost a lot, but where your time is an investment and your well-being benefits. Take a walk with a friend, rather than meeting for lunch. Cook at home and invite people over. Ask them to bring the wine. The pleasure here is in the time spent, not the bill.

Look at doing a home exchange for your summer vacation. That's one of the best-kept secrets that the hotel industry doesn't want you to find out about. Forget Airbnb. This is exchanging homes with peers, where no money changes hands. Don't worry about what someone would do to your home. Ask yourself what you would do to theirs. Just as you wouldn't travel to Colorado with your family to burgle someone, neither would they. Join a membership association and start planning.

Abundance is about the experience and mindset of enjoyment. Sometimes that's about a splurge, a really nice hotel, or ordering whatever you want on the menu. But more often it's about who you are with, the conversation and laughter, being aware of the time together, and really appreciating it. Why else would anyone ever go camping?

Look to the Horizon

When you're planning your life and thinking of your career as just one piece in the puzzle, it helps to look out longer term. Earlier in this book, we did some long-range planning to see where you'd like to be and what kind of life you'd like to be living. The challenge with creating new habits is that they support our future self and are hard on our current self, who is reluctant to change and finds it hard.

Rationally, we know we need to simply start doing the things we have identified as necessary to the life we want. But we are emotional creatures and dislike change, even when the current situation is unsatisfactory. It's familiar and that has a value all of its own.

Make it easier for you to change the habits of a lifetime by building in as much support and reward as you can. Keep the bar low on your own expectations and see if you can vault over them.

Six ways to keep yourself on track when implementing change

1. Find an image that captures what you're striving for and tack it above your desk or on your fridge.
2. Put the tasks you want to achieve on your calendar, not just on your to-do list. If you have to move them, re-schedule them.

3. Plan rewards, small or large, for accomplishing what you set out to do. If you finish in less time, take a break. Don't add something else.

4. Don't add too many new habits all at once. Get one going well, and then add another. It generally takes 21 days for a habit to stick.

5. Find someone who is completely supportive and tell him or her how you're doing, or not doing. You want encouragement, not problemsolving. You may need to tell them that.

6. Schedule check-ins with yourself to evaluate how you're doing against your goals. Put the check-ins on your calendar and pull out the notebook or file where you jotted them down. Spend an hour reflecting on your progress.

Keeping your focus on the longer-term goal is critically important. It's the small efforts every day that will get you there. The small efforts become habits, which require less effort and over time result in achievement.

I didn't get there by wishing for it or hoping for it, but by working for it. —Estee Lauder

Stay focused but also remember to give yourself a break. There is no point in beating yourself up for what you didn't do. Make a note of what you got done. I have a friend who is a highly successful expert in sales and who keeps a journal to record what she accomplished at the end of each day. It makes her feel a lot better than focusing on what didn't get done.

If you set yourself three tasks for the day and can get those done, or well started, that's a successful day. There will always be more things on the list.

The following is some good advice I was once given: Write down all the things you'd like to do today. Ask yourself which items will move you forward and which are most time-sensitive? Pick one of each and then one more. Get those three done, and then give yourself a reward.

You're building infrastructure and support for the longer term. Each day counts toward the goal.

5

Whose Highlight Reel?

In a nutshell: Comparing yourself to others can be toxic and undermine all your efforts. Don't forget you are watching only the highlight reel of someone else's life, while you live the "no holds barred" documentary of your own. Confidence is the secret sauce to changing the normative pressure that surrounds you. This chapter explores how to be purposeful about creating reinforcements for your vision.

Mirror, Mirror on the Wall

Lucia had recently left a senior position at an investment house. A merger was in the works and there had been a round of layoffs, followed by a round of voluntary redundancies. She took the redundancy package when offered because she felt it was time for a change but also because the planning around the merger had been particularly fraught. Everyone had to reapply for a new position, even if it was the one they currently held. It was clear there would be fewer positions than previously.

The communication from management had been lacking, to put it mildly. Instead, the water cooler internal communications function kicked into high gear and soon everyone was living in a world of rumor and counter-rumor. Colleagues were being coy about whether they were being shortlisted and called to interview. For many, not being called to interview, while others were, was the way they found out they were losing their jobs. No one knew whom to trust or whom to believe. Lucia found it extremely depressing and demoralizing. So she decided to leave and look for a new role in a different organization. The redundancy package helped soften the anxiety of being unemployed, initially.

She soon found herself getting anxious again when weeks passed and things were moving slowly. She had hired a coach and knew rationally that it would take a few months to find a role at her level. She also knew that she was doing all the right things: reaching out to contacts, placing calls, meeting people, networking at industry conferences, and telling everyone she knew that she was looking for a new opportunity. So why the anxiety, besides the obvious impatience to be done with job searching?

Much of her anxiety came from talking to former colleagues who had also left and were job hunting. They all seemed to have more leads than she did. They seemed much more confident about their prospects. Some were more senior to her in the old organization and were applying for the same positions she was at other firms. Surely they were better placed to succeed?

The problem was she was only watching the highlight reel of their efforts—the positive snapshots they provided of what was happening. Her former colleagues only talked about the success they had and the successes they anticipated (but hadn't yet materialized). They weren't telling her about their nagging doubts, the anxiety they felt about the redundancy package running out, or the pressure at home and tension the job hunt was causing in their relationships. They weren't talking about existing pressures now exacerbated with difficult teenage children or aging parents. And that senior colleague applying for the same job didn't mention his anxiety at being much older, paler, and male competing with a younger Hispanic woman like Lucia.

Meanwhile, in her life she was living the no holds barred documentary of every minor rejection, every phone call not returned, and the energy needed to show up at that industry conference as simply herself, without the shield of being from a company.

The following are four things Lucia did to keep her confidence up while job hunting.

1. **Logging accomplishments at the end of the day in a journal.** Listing all the things she had done made Lucia feel better when progress

wasn't evident. She had been making an effort, and it was important to remind herself of that.

2. **Spending a specific, limited amount of time job hunting.** Lucia worked on finding a job every morning for two hours, placing calls and submitting applications. Then she called it a day. Working eight-hour days won't increase your chances of finding a job.

3. **Meeting as many relevant people as possible.** Formatting and reformatting your resume won't make the difference in your job hunt, but meeting people who can help you will. Lucia was diligent about reaching out and setting up meetings with people who could help her or refer her to new positions.

4. **Enjoying the time off.** Lucia made a conscious effort to enjoy not working, knowing it would be temporary. She did some things she wouldn't normally do, like visiting a museum for lunch with a friend, taking a yoga class in the middle of the day, and hanging out with her kids after school.

Confidence Factor

Confidence: *noun con·fi·dence \\'kän-fə-dən(t)s—A feeling or consciousness of one's powers or of reliance on one's circumstances.*

Ironically, what was happening in the previous example was that Lucia was witnessing her former colleagues' confidence and wilting in the face of it. We will ignore whether or not it was misplaced confidence on their part and if they were simply exhibiting bravado to cover their true concerns.

It wasn't until she increased her own confidence that she was able to have some perspective and realize she was doing just fine. It's a complete trope to say that confidence can only come from within. Confidence can be learned, borrowed, and bought!

Lucia hired me as a coach for this period in her life because she knew she needed expert advice on managing her transition and negotiating the contract of her next role. What she didn't realize was that she was also getting a cheerleader-in-chief.

Having someone who was squarely on her side, with no agenda other than to help her was exactly what Lucia needed. I was able to give her perspective on the process and reassure her that she was doing the right thing. I was also able to convey my own confidence in her abilities and her prospects so that they became her own. In effect, Lucia was buying some confidence and learning to maintain it.

If confidence is a critical factor in your success, what are you doing to ensure you've got enough? See if you can answer the following questions.

- Who can give you sound, unbiased advice?
- Who provides you with unadulterated support and enthusiasm?

- Who is your biggest fan?
- Who is a leader in your field and thinks highly of you?
- Who leaves you feeling energized and confident?
- Are you spending enough time with these people?

If you're in a transition or trying to make changes to your life, it's important to build your confidence. Finding ways to do that can be fun.

Confidence is often found in the reflection of ourselves from others, but it matters who those people are. If a small child thinks you're a great baker, that's nice. But if a professional cook loves your cupcakes, that's much more meaningful. Seek out people who you admire and get their perspectives on what you're trying to do and how you're going about it. That's where a colleague, mentor, or professional coach can help.

It also helps to have the unadulterated support of at least some family and friends. One of the hardest things in life is to persevere when the person you're closest with doesn't have confidence in your ability to succeed. Behind every successful entrepreneur are good friends and spouses who believed in them when things were at their most dire.

Be explicit with your spouse or partner that you need support and that without his or her confidence in you, it's hard to have confidence in yourself. If they still can't do that, you know where you stand.

It's easier with friends. Be selective. Not all friends can provide the confidence you need to feed off of. You can still play tennis with your negative buddy, but stop confiding your anxieties to him. It's only getting you down. Focus on the game with him, but make sure you're also spending time with your biggest fans.

Doing things for others is a great way to boost our own confidence. There are always people worse off than ourselves, and being able to help someone gives us a feeling of competence and control that leaks over to the rest of our lives. It may sound the opposite of altruistic, but there is much to be gained by volunteering with a charity or helping out a neighbor.

Spend time with people who are doing what you want to be doing. You'll start to notice something. You are probably just as smart as they are. Maybe they've just been doing it longer and are more confident in their abilities because it has been validated more often. You can learn to do this and build your own confidence.

Be deliberate in finding ways to boost your confidence and maintain it. Think of self-confidence as a plant that needs regular watering to thrive.

Normative Pressure

Facebook is the ultimate highlight reel. If you spend any time there at all, you become convinced that everyone else is living a much better existence than you. It's an endless litany of fun lunches and family gatherings, graduations and awards. Everyone is laughing and raising a glass. It's nonstop fun.

If you keep comparing yourself to this bunch, you'll end up miserable. A couple of things to keep in mind to gain perspective:

1. **People only post what they want you to see on Facebook.** They don't post about the rows with their spouses or the promotions they didn't get.

2. **You're looking at the selected edits of tens or hundreds of people compressed into one stream.** It's like an end-of-year wrap-up of the best movies of the year. It seems like a long list now, but there was nothing to watch in February.

It's really hard to flow against the current. If social pressure gets you down, you have to try to step back and maintain perspective.

I know a successfully published author who is married to a journalist. Both are highly accomplished in their fields and enjoy what they do. They have three adorable children who are all healthy and sound. Life sounds good, right? But they live in New York City and compared to their friends and neighbors, they are as poor as church mice. Everyone around them seems to be earning multiples of what they do and are not concerned at all about finances. Instead, their friends agonize about which private school their children should attend and which caterer to use for their holiday parties. By comparison, my friends are anxious about credit card debt and how they will pay for an increase in their condo maintenance.

If they lived in another part of the country, they would be considered affluent, part of the 1 percent, but in New York the 1 percent starts stratospheres above them.

Sometimes it's hard to remember when you've got it good.

Reports on the happiest countries are highly revealing. The top 10 ranked countries in 2016 were Denmark, Switzerland, Iceland, Norway, Finland, Canada, the Netherlands, New Zealand, Australia, and Sweden.[1]

The United States came in 13th, just ahead of Costa Rica and Puerto Rico. China was 83rd and India 118th, while poor war-torn Burundi in Africa came in last of more than 150 countries.

The hallmarks of the happiest countries are relatively low levels of inequality and strong social safety nets. As inequality increases, unhappiness does too. This makes sense if we look at my friends in New York.

If they were surrounded by people of the same income, they would likely feel relatively well off. They both love their jobs and are rewarded and recognized for what they do. They have a strong circle of friends and active social lives. The main wrinkle is this feeling that they are doing less well than everyone else and falling behind. It's the relative inequality compared to the lives around them and the expense of living in a city with so many wealthy people that distorts their view.

We tend to look up to compare how we are doing against those doing better, rather than down to see how much better off we are than most. But continually looking up gives you a crick in your neck and a distorted view of the world.

Becky is a teacher and married to Noah, who is also a teacher. She came from a wealthy family and always assumed she would marry someone who made more than her. She didn't. She met Noah, fell in love, and stayed in love. She adores her job, teaching history at a private prep school in Connecticut. She is highly respected in her field. She is surrounded by neighbors who are lawyers and bankers. Her street is lined with parked Volvos and BMWs. As a couple, she and Noah earn a fraction of what some of their neighbors earn.

But Becky appreciates what they have that their neighbors don't. Although they work long hours during term time, they have six weeks off in the summer and other long holidays during the year. As a couple, they have an afternoon off during the week when neither of them have classes. That's a date afternoon. Their two boys attend the same school at reduced tuition, so they all share a morning and afternoon commute and see each other during the day.

"I love it and wouldn't have it any other way," said Becky. "There were years when I was envious of other people's existence and carefree approach to money, but I love the life we have created. It's special, and I'm grateful for it."

Especially for Girls

The highlight reel is especially insidious for women. The pressure to conform to an unrealistic societal image starts early. Little girls are praised for being good and nice, for being pretty and sweet. Meanwhile, boys are rewarded for bravery and risk-taking. Boys have their own issues in terms of being pressured not to reveal their emotions or weaknesses, but those are not my concern here.

Women grow up not even realizing the pressures they are under. The teenage years bring angst about changing body shape, ideals of beauty shaped by stick-like models on catwalks, and pouting celebrities dressed in outfits that would result in streetwalking citations or a nasty cold for the rest of us.

Throughout school and then in the workplace, women are penalized for being outspoken, called on less, and less likely to be offered difficult assignments. Women who break the rules are penalized by other women as often as they are by men. They are labeled a bitch, often on wheels (which I have never understood), pushy, bossy, shrewish, and so on.

Although things are changing, progress has been painfully slow. Women still earn about 20 percent less than men for the same work.[2] The number of women leading Fortune 500 companies has actually dropped and in 2016 hovered at 4 percent.[3] And what seems like progress often isn't. Longitudinal studies now show that when women start moving into professions in large numbers, the average pay in those professions starts to decline.[4] How depressing is that?

All of these factors result in women not having sufficient role models for how to be successful in the workplace and, at the same time, being bombarded with unrealistic images of how they should be, look, and act.

Somewhere along the way it became acceptable to suggest that if women just tried harder they could succeed at work while also being a domestic goddess, doting mother, and hot babe (MILF?). This theory failed to acknowledge the complete lack of systemic support for women and families. That support is regularly found in European countries and, ironically, also in developing countries for middle-class professionals, at the very least.

Women in America need to give themselves a break or move to Sweden. In fact, most countries in Europe, including far poorer countries such as the Ukraine, provide free or subsidized child care that actually starts when women go back to work.[5] The United States is also the rare exception to a global norm of legally mandated maternity leave. It stands in lonely solidarity with Papua New Guinea as the only two countries in the world that don't guarantee paid leave for new mothers.[6]

Meanwhile, in many developing countries women are making much more rapid progress professionally than men, simply because the overall rate of economic growth is higher, so there are more opportunities for everyone. Middle-class professionals in poor countries often have much more household help and support than women in wealthier countries because of the low cost of labor.[7]

It's a myth, by the way, that Europeans are taxed at much higher rates than Americans in order to make this family support affordable. Europeans pay only slightly higher income taxes than Americans do, while Swedes and Britons pay less, and all get far more in return.[8]

Women in the United States constantly blame themselves for not trying harder, and being able to do more at work and home with much less support than their counterparts elsewhere. Meanwhile, they read yet another story featuring an airbrushed wonder woman who is finding a cure for cancer while competing in triathlons, raising four kids, and setting up orphanages abroad.

To make any change happen, we need to pester our legislators to improve conditions for families and support each other in challenging norms of behavior. Something as simple as supporting another woman's point in a meeting, a technique adopted by female partners in a major law firm, can help.

We would all do well to abide by Secretary Madeleine Albright's admonishment that "There is a special place in hell for women who do not support other women."

Create Your Own Highlight Reel

A coaching client of mine was invited to a party in Los Angeles. It was an industry event for media and entertainment companies, and the most senior people in her organization were attending. She spent the evening networking, caught up with former colleagues, and at one point found herself sitting next to Steven Spielberg. It was a pretty good evening.

Yet, throughout the event she was anxious and out of sorts. She had been invited at the last minute and wasn't part of the original delegation from her company. When she arrived, although they had her name on the list of attendees, there hadn't been time to produce a pre-printed name badge, so she ended up with a hand-written one. She felt this called attention to the fact that she had not been included originally.

Although she was pleased to be there, she kept mulling over why she hadn't been thought of initially. She said it reminded her of childhood and not being part of the in-crowd at school or in her neighborhood.

Now she is hanging out with Steven Spielberg but she feels snubbed and like she's not really part of the "cool crew."

By contrast, many years ago I ran an event for Delta Air Lines in London as their head of international corporate communications. I had neglected to finalize the company name for an attendee. Although his name badge had his correct name, it listed the company he worked for as "TBC," as in "to be confirmed." I was terribly embarrassed but he thought it was hilarious and started to joke that maybe it stood for something cool like "The Big Cheese."

Contrast these two experiences and you'll find similarities in what happened, but differences in the reaction of the individual. My client was wrapped up in her own experience of how she was reading the situation, even though rationally she knew it was great that she was there and that the event had gone well.

Sometimes we need to create our own highlight reel. If we focus too much on what's not working, what's yet to be done, or what isn't as we planned, we can end up mired in all of the negatives. Our mind has a tendency to focus on negative things because its primary job is to warn us about bad stuff. It's very important that we notice the saber-toothed tiger than the sunset, as Dan Gilbert would say.[9] The only downside is that we are always scanning for the saber-toothed tiger and miss the sunset in the process.

Exercise: Do a quick and dirty inventory of your highlights:

1. *Things I am good at*
2. *Successes I have had*
3. *Positive ways people describe me*
4. *Things I enjoy doing*
5. *Obstacles I have surmounted*

Now you have your own highlight reel. These are the best things about you. When you feel tempted to compare yourself to others, whip this out to remind yourself of how you're doing so far. It's probably pretty good.

One easy way to create your own highlight reel is to actually capture the highlights. A technique pioneered by Martin Seligman is to notice what went well and why at the end of each day.[10] He recommends writing down at the end of the day three things that went well and why they went well. For example, you might note that a meeting went well that day because you had prepared for it or because your workplace nemesis wasn't there.

He also suggests that couples ask each other that question and that parents ask it of their children at the end of the day. The act of recalling what went well and why allows us to relive the positive experience and also to see the things that contributed to it. In the previous example, that would be either effort or luck. It is a much richer interaction than "How was your day?" followed by "Fine."

Seligman suggests we use the technique when we want to really listen to people and appreciate what they experienced. It also prevents us from slipping into problem-solving or starting to compare it with what happened to us. Rarely a good idea!

WWWW is the short form for "what went well and why." Post it somewhere to remind yourself. Try it at your next family dinner or begin a journal to record the highlights of your day just before you drift off to sleep. You'll be pressing play on a highlight reel for your subconscious self—much better than watching the no holds barred documentary.

6

Relationships That Rapidly Propel

In a nutshell: Supportive relationships are key to your success, and time spent in unproductive ones takes away from what's really important. Figuring out who does what in your relationship map will help bring you clarity. It will make it easier to reduce the time spent with people who bring you down and spend more time with the people who really matter to you.

The Ties That Bind

Our relationships with others are very diverse. They run the gamut from casual to essential, from neutral to passionate, and from supportive to destructive. They also change over time. We ourselves change over time, and our needs and desires are often different at various points in our life.

We tend to weigh ourselves down with relationships we stay in for far too long that no longer fulfill any need. But it's extremely hard to extricate ourselves from them. They cover our lives like thickly growing ivy on a house that we don't even notice after a while.

I know a number of people who realized that they were in friendships that had run their course and no longer provided any pleasure. In some cases, both sides made an effort to re-ignite what had once been an important relationship. But these attempts were invariably out of sync and couldn't halt a natural evolution. The basis of the relationship was no longer there. They needed to walk away.

Instead, they would meet up, have unsatisfying conversations and schedule another lunch or dinner, often canceling the appointment several times to put off what would not be a fun event in lives that were short of free time.

They epitomized *The New Yorker* cartoon by Robert Mankoff of a man standing in his office making an appointment with someone over the phone:

"No, Thursday's out. How about never—is never good for you?"[1]

We all do this. We spend time with people when we really don't want to and don't get enough time with others we thoroughly enjoy. Sometimes it's about honoring a value we have around family, loyalty, or commitments. We go to see that aging uncle because we think it's important to take care of people in their old age, even though it's a drag to get out to him and the trip takes up half the day.

We sometimes do things we don't want to, a secondary choice, in order to support something that's really important, a primary choice. In this case traveling to visit that uncle is a secondary choice, because it supports our value around caring for elderly relatives, the primary choice.

What's interesting is that in both cases we are making a choice. We don't have to visit that uncle. Lots of people don't visit their elderly relatives. Knowing that it's a choice relieves the sense of burden and we now enjoy the trip because we remember why we are doing it: to support a value that is important to us.

But what about the other relationships, the ones in which there is no higher value being served? Why do we continue to spend time with people who bring us down or simply don't bring anything? These are the ties that bind, in a bad way.

Often the hardest of these ties to change are the familial ones. It's easy for me to suggest you stop spending time with people who bring you down, but what if that person is your mother?

You're not alone in having difficult relationships with people you still have to see or want to see, be they siblings, parents, or other family members. One way to approach it is to have a relationship with them as they are and stop wishing they would be different.

That means adjusting your expectations to the reality of the people you're dealing with. They have probably been consistent in their behavior for years, yet you still expect them to be someone else. Try having a relationship with them based in the reality of who they are. That might mean finally cutting back the amount of time you see them or speak with them. Or it might mean changing the subject so you don't end up so furious after time spent with them. If you want to maintain the relationship, find something you can enjoy together, cut out the rest, and remember you're making a choice.

Map the Landscape

When I worked at the World Bank, I was responsible for external communications at its private sector investment arm, the International Finance Corporation (IFC). The IFC's mandate was to support economic growth and job creation in developing countries. It did this by investing in businesses large and small around the world and by encouraging other investors to join in financing those businesses. Many of these companies were operating in very tough environments where regular banks didn't want to lend.

Often, the projects they wanted to finance were long-term infrastructure investments that needed patient capital and plenty of expertise to manage their environmental and social impact. That's where the IFC came in. It didn't need to make a quick return on its investment, and it had world-class experts to help mitigate the impact of large pipelines and power plants.

The environmental issues were often challenging, like making sure the water that comes out of a pulp and paper plant into a local river is as clean or cleaner than the water that went into it upstream. But the social issues were just as important. It was imperative to make sure that the local communities were not adversely impacted by a project and that they benefited in some way.

Often, that was in the form of jobs and being part of the "supply chain" to the project. If the local towns and villages could provide labor, food, or transport services to the plant, the company would save money by not importing from the capital and the locals benefit from increased incomes. This was especially important in remote communities where jobs were few and far between. It also meant that relations between the company and the local community were based on a mutual interdependence and likely to be constructive. Many companies had seen the cost of not having good relations with local communities in the form of sabotage, protests, and road blockages that could shut a plant down and cost the company millions of dollars.

To make sure they got this right, the social and environmental experts at the IFC would draw up what they called a "stakeholder map." This was a document that catalogued all of the different groups impacted by the project in some way. This could include everyone from the central government to local councils or village elders, residents, farmers, workers, activist groups, religious organizations, local businesses, and schools. They were called stakeholders and each was impacted differently by the project and had a different level of influence. Some were loud and vocal but not actually affected by the project, and others could be easily overlooked but would be significantly impacted or should stand to benefit from the project.

The experts at the IFC would "map" the stakeholders to make sure they understood the scale of the impact on them and make sure no one was being overlooked and that the relationships with each were being appropriately managed.

You are not trying to manage the impact of a hydroelectric power plant in Africa, but surprisingly the same approach works just as well with your relationships.

You can map the quality of your relationships against their importance to you. That will help you see where you should be spending your time.

If it helps to think about influence rather than importance, do that. Many of our professional relationships are easier to see through this lens. You'll also notice that some people may not seem important, but they have outsize influence; take the assistant to your boss, for example and look at the sample on page 121 that I have created.

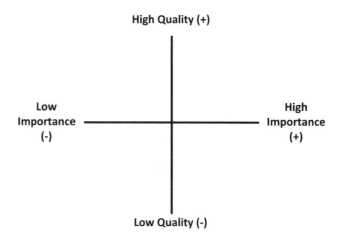

Now place the people in your life in one of those four quadrants. Some will have high influence and you have a good relationship. That's great. With others you have a great relationship but they are not very influential. For example, I love my mail carrier, Brian, and he is fond of me, but ultimately he doesn't impact my life that much. You'll hopefully find any truly hostile people in the lower-left quadrant, low quality of relationship and low influence.

Now bring your attention to whoever is in the top left quadrant. These are the people with whom you don't have a great relationship but they have influence over your life. This is where you have work to do. You ideally want to move them into the top right corner. Think about the ways you might improve your relationship with them or, if that seems unlikely, see if you can remove yourself from their orbit to reduce their influence.

Values Come in Tiers

Companies talk a lot nowadays about their values. There is an entire industry in helping companies figure out their values and develop mission statements. There is a belief that articulating key elements of your corporate culture helps employees be more engaged and productive.

Companies also use things like mission statements and values to impress upon customers what they stand for. Google has the "Google Truths," for example. The truths include statements like: "Focus on the user and all else will follow," "It's best to do one thing really, really well," and "You can be serious without a suit."[2] GE has Growth Values: external focus, clear thinker, imagination and courage, inclusiveness and expertise. And Mars Incorporated has Five Principals: quality, responsibility, mutuality, efficiency, and freedom.

Issues arise for companies when the stated values are not what employees or customers experience. It's fair to say that companies like Enron and Countrywide Financial had values they proclaimed to adhere to and patently didn't. In the fall of 2016, Wells Fargo was fined $185 million for fraudulently opening millions of accounts customers didn't ask for or need. Yet, Wells Fargo proclaims that "ethics" and "what's right for customers" are two of its five core values. When employees know that the corporate culture internally doesn't match up with what is espoused externally, it creates conflict and generally customers experience that conflict. It's hard to fake a corporate culture.

The same thing is true for individuals. You are much better off when you are aware of your personal values and they align with what you're doing professionally. If not, you experience the same sense of conflict as those employees inside a company where the values are not reflected in reality.

The following is an exercise to discover your values. This is much easier with a partner.

Exercise: *Jot down five things that are very important to you. Then, taking one of the five things at a time, ask yourself why they are important. For each answer, ask why is that important, and again for that answer ask why it is important until you get to a dead end and are answering "It just is."*

Here's an example. If "money" is one of the things you list as important to you, ask why. You might have a number of different answers that lead you to a different underlying value.

Person #1

- Pick one of the five things that is important to you: *Money.*
- Why is money important to you? *So I can take care of my family.*
- Why is it important to take care of your family? *Because I want them to be well taken care of and for us to be able to do what we want.*
- Why is that important to you? *Because I want us to have choices.*
- Why is that important? *It's really important to have control and freedom to choose what we do.*
- Do you think that's a core value for you? *Yes.*
- What is a word or phrase that expresses that value? *Freedom.*

For someone else the same word could lead in a different direction.

Person #2

- Pick one of the five things that are important to you: *Money.*
- Why is money important to you? *I don't want to worry about it.*
- Why is it important to you not to worry about money? *Because I don't like to worry about not having enough money.*

- Why is that important to you? *Because I like to feel secure and know I can pay for what I need.*
- Why is that important? *Because I like to know I will be okay even if things change.*
- Do you think that's a core value for you? *Yes.*
- What is a word or phrase that expresses that value? *Security.*

Figuring out your values is a really useful exercise because it can shed light on why you have difficulty in some relationships compared to others. Often when we get into conflict with others, it's because our values are not aligned.

For example, if our boss drops something on us at the last minute we will react differently if we value structure or enjoy spontaneity. For some people it's enormously stressful to have their workday derailed and for others it gives an energy boost and feeling of being useful. Obviously how the request is made also plays a big role.

Look back at your relationship map and see how some of those difficult relationships might be due to differing values. It's not that you should only have relationships with people who are likeminded in terms of values, but it helps us understand why things go wrong when values are not aligned.

If you find that you're working in an environment with very different values to the ones you hold, recognize that it can be very stressful. It's not easy for you to change your values, and why would you? But it's even harder to change the values of the organization around you. You can either make your peace with these differences or look to make a move.

Leader Profile: Elizabeth Vazquez

Elizabeth Vazquez has always been clear about what she wanted to do, and it was informed by how she grew up.

"I was born in Mexico and brought up in Arizona, raised by a single mom. We had very little money. It was so hard. I learned empathy for the role many women have: trying to take care of their families."

Elizabeth is the president, CEO, and cofounder of WEConnect International, a nonprofit that helps women-owned businesses in 100 countries sell into the supply chains of some of the largest companies in the world, including Walmart, Johnson & Johnson, and Exxon Mobil.

"I remember being teased for being Mexican at school in Arizona and coming home crying to my mom, who said, "Well, you are Mexican." I saw first-hand how people can make assumptions about you and be prejudiced against you."

Elizabeth learned early on not to accept other people's assumptions about her and not to let them limit her from doing what she wanted to do. Her very first job offer was from the U.S. government. She convinced the hiring manager that the work she really wanted to do was very different from the job available but equally valuable, and so the vacancy was adapted to fit her, not the other way around.

"In my career, I've always wanted to leave the world a better place and to have had a positive impact. I learned from my mother not to complain, but to get out and fight for what you care about. I remember going to protests with her at a very early age."

Elizabeth says she always tries to do work she cares about with people she cares about. As well as running WEConnect International, Elizabeth is a member of the United Nations High Level Panel on Women's Economic Empowerment, which includes heads of state, heads of corporations, and heads of multinationals.

She sits on a number of boards and is an advisor to many more.

How does she get so much done? "I am very particular about what I agree to do and only commit to things that fit with furthering women's empowerment. I am very good at delegating and have surrounded myself with smart, competent, passionate people."

"My advice to younger people is to think about your reputation because it is with you forever. Being collaborative, supportive, making real contributions, that's what counts. People remember what you do."

With teams in 21 countries, Elizabeth travels a lot. She says that being home with her young daughter and husband is where she gets her energy back. "That's my place to relax, celebrate, heal, physically being around them. They ground me."

Sponsors and Mentors

Sponsors and mentors are different, and you need both. A mentor is someone senior to you at your company (or in another organization), to whom you go to for advice. They don't have supervisory responsibility for you.

A sponsor is someone senior who supports you in your career and can take action directly on your behalf or lobby for you to be promoted or be given new assignments. They may be your supervisor or above you in the reporting line. Or they may be outside your reporting line but have authority in the business.

A mentor is really helpful but a sponsor has more power. That's why it's important to have both.

Many firms now have formal mentoring programs. If those exist, check them out and see if colleagues have found them valuable. If the mentoring program holds events, these can be useful places for networking with peers and senior colleagues alike.

In formal programs, you may choose your mentor or they may be assigned to you. That can work out well or not. As the mentee, you need to be the one to reach out and be persistent in setting up time to meet with your mentor. Bring specific issues to those meetings; ask them about what they learned in the course of their career and so on. As the mentor, you always gain far more than you think in these relationships and often more than the mentee!

You see the company from a different perspective, gain intelligence about what's happening in other parts of the organization, and ensure that your own network expands rather than shrinks over time.

A mentor/mentee relationship is like a friendship with an older sibling except it's at work, and you like them.

Sponsorship is a different kettle of fish. Here you are building a relationship with someone who can promote you, protect you, and progress your career. It's almost like an artist having a patron. As the person being sponsored, your job is to be loyal and to make them look good whenever you can. Their job is to nurture talent that's loyal to them and good for the company.

That can sometimes get out of whack when the goals of the sponsor are not aligned with the goals of the company. Then you end up with tribes loyal to different patrons who themselves are squabbling and using the members of their tribes as pawns in internecine corporate warfare.

But let's assume that's not the case where you work.

Do you have a sponsor already? Does your boss act as your sponsor or not? Who might be a good sponsor for you?

The sponsor–sponsored relationship isn't always explicit. There is more upside to it than with a mentor, as it can result in promotions, pay increases, increased responsibility, and so on. There is also plenty more downside risk associated with sponsorship. That means when your sponsor is doing well, you may be doing well; but when they are not, you go down with them.

I knew a global media company in New York where patronage was well established and people were identified as belonging to one or another of half a dozen senior players. Colleagues would be identified as being "one of Michael's people," and the like. Whenever a top patron was toppled in a reshuffle, an entire team of people below them would go also, or find themselves in much diminished roles.

Map out your mentors and sponsors. Use an x/y axis like the one on page 121 to track the level of influence of your mentors and sponsors and the quality of your relationship with them. Make sure you have some people in that top right quadrant: high-influence and high-quality relationships!

Purposeful Networking

Coaching clients of mine frequently tell me they hate networking. They think it's a waste of time. They despise the people who do it a lot. They think it's about politics and sucking up. They think it's about golf.

Here is why networking is important: It's part of your job. For those of you who think you don't have time to network, it actually makes you more effective and allows you to do more in less time. Think about it. You can get more done if you have strong relationships across a wide swathe of the business than if you are a stranger at the other end of an email exchange.

You can work across teams for which you don't have authority more easily. You can get intelligence and advice more quickly. And you can navigate bumps and disagreements more successfully when you know people well and they know and trust you. All of that makes you more valuable to the business and better able to contribute.

So now that you're over that hurdle, who should you be networking with?

The single most important aspect of professional networking is being purposeful about it. Networking is about having a network of strong relationships, not about golf. You need to think about why you want to network and that will help you figure out how. What's your objective? Do you want credit for your team for something they did? Do you need more resources? Want a promotion?

Write down your objective. Now make a list of the people who need to be influenced on that issue. That's your target audience. Now expand it a little by listing some of the key people who influence them. Don't forget that these can be their subordinates. Look for gatekeepers like administrative assistants and resource holders like budget officers. This expanded group is your target audience. Keep them in mind. Now let's move on to how to network.

Don't overthink it. Build relationships. Provide value. Brag a little. That's all you need to do. Be clear and straightforward about what you're doing.

Find out what's on the other person's agenda. Ask them what they are having difficulty with and see if you can help. Find out what's important to them and remember to ask about that.

Provide something of value, some intelligence from your side of the business, a relevant article you've read, or something practical that they need or would appreciate.

Women, stop asking your male colleagues about their families. That may be a good way to build a relationship with some female colleagues, but you're generally better off asking guys what they're working on. Then brag a little. Men think this is completely normal. That's why they brag so often to you.

Don't worry about how it comes across. Tell them about some minor coup or about how well your team did this quarter. Say "we" in your statements if you're worried about being too boastful.

Show up early at events and receptions. Force yourself to talk to some of the people in your targeted group. Ask them about themselves, give them something of value, drop in some facts about the good stuff you're doing, then go home. You've been networking. Job done.

7

Building a Personal Brand

I n a nutshell: Building a personal brand reinforces your aspirations. It's critical that you look and act the part you want to play. This isn't about simply faking it until you make it. This is about purposefully building your visibility and cultivating your presence. It's about getting external validation to promote yourself at work, and beginning to live the life to which you aspire.

Defining Your Brand

Christine Lagarde enters the press conference room at the IMF exactly at 10 a.m. It is two days before the annual meetings of the IMF and World Bank. Hundreds of government officials, bankers, and ministers of finance have gathered in Washington, D.C., to discuss the state of the global economy. She moves purposefully toward the stage with a smile of recognition to familiar faces and takes her seat.

She is tall and slim, in her 50s, with closely cropped gray hair and a year-round tan. She is wearing tailored black pants, a fitted jacket, and a colored scarf at her throat. Her earrings are discreet and look expensive. The speakers on either side of her are men in suits and ties. They look faded and tired and dressed so uniformly as to be interchangeable.

After an introduction, she begins her speech. She tells the audience that she wants them to remember three points from her remarks. She tells them what the three points are. She discusses the three points in detail, adding statistics and examples to make her case.

Her tone is friendly but firm. She alternates smiling with a serious gaze. She concludes by reminding the audience of the three points and then takes questions. She is humorous and slightly irreverent while taking questions, self-deprecating and warm in her manner. Hostile questioners are treated with the utmost politeness and an offer to discuss further outside the press conference. Whether that discussion actually happens is another matter but the audience is charmed and on her side now, even if the questioner is not.

Christine Lagarde has a very strong personal brand. She deals with the most serious financial issues in the world at any point in time: the Eurozone crisis, the Greek default,

U.S. Fed policy, the China slow-down, and others. Yet, she is always a calm and measured presence. People expect her to be pragmatic and constructive, to be crystal clear in her pronouncements. And she is. That is her brand.

Her brand is also elegance. She dresses well, conservatively but very elegant. She is a minimalist, carrying at most a well-made handbag. No piles of papers or large tote. She is often the only woman in a sea of suited men. The annual photograph of her with the board members of IMF is comical for its gender imbalance. Yet she looks comfortable as if with a group of classmates at a college reunion. This is all part of her brand.

What's your brand? How would people describe you? We are talking about the attributes people ascribe to you, not just your appearance. How do people experience you?

Exercise: *Jot down the five key characteristics that you think people associate with you, positive or negative. For example, they might say you are warm, reserved, quiet, boisterous, skeptical, informed, curious, kind, solitary, forthright, calm, enthusiastic, ambitious, passionate, and more.*

Now do a reality check. Having asked for their help, hand three good friends or colleagues a blank index card and ask them to write down the first five adjectives that come to mind when they think of you, positive and negative. No discussing. Be sure to say you want honest answers and no filtering. Compare the lists.

Are you happy with what you've got? You might be pleasantly surprised at how people perceive you. I remember being taken aback at how many people find me warm and enthusiastic. I think I can be quite critical and judgmental. That was not their perception.

Now let's look at this from a professional point of view. Are any of these attributes less helpful in the workplace? Are you reserved to the point of invisible? Is your flexibility perceived as not being convinced of your own opinions? How do you want to be perceived in the work-place? Do you want to be known as boisterous and fun in the office?

Exercise: *Jot down the attributes you would like people to associate with you, but which they don't currently. For example, approachable, successful, elegant, calm, generous, smart, and so on.*

Put these aspirational traits on an index card. Now add the most common traits your friends and colleagues used to describe you. Put green circles around the positive traits and red circles around the negative ones. Post the card on your bulletin board.

You can strengthen or change your own personal brand by being aware of how people experience you and deciding to develop the traits to which you aspire. You can do this with behaviors, your presence, and even your appearance. The key is a conscious decision to amplify or restrain some of those characteristics. Start practicing being the brand you want to be.

Appearance is not the sum of your brand, just as a logo is the not the sum of a company's brand. But it is an important part. What can you do to amplify the positive in your appearance?

Good grooming lies at the heart of a good appearance. That means nails manicured, shoes polished, shirt ironed, and hair regularly trimmed. Once you've got the basics down, apply the exercise of aspiration.

How would you like to appear? Do you need to lose a couple of pounds or get a new winter coat?

My rule of thumb is always to dress up rather than down, especially for work, but even at social events. This advice is hard earned, as I found myself too often at meetings in a T-shirt without a jacket and at church services clad in denim, feeling uncomfortable because everyone else was dressed much more formally.

For women, make sure you have a small number of high-quality basic items in your wardrobe: stylish jackets, tailored black pants, a nice winter coat, and formal shoes. Add dark-blue designer jeans, some white tailored shirts and black T-shirts, and you're done. You don't have to have suits if they are not worn where you work, but if you do, invest in a few good ones and take care of them. A good bag and shoes will carry you a long way.

For men, get the basics. That means three suits, 10 shirts, two blazers, three pair of shoes, two belts, three trousers, 10 pair of socks, and five ties. Think Tom Ford or Daniel Craig. There are plenty of role models out there. Look at the men in your office, leaders you admire, and men in public life. Who looks good? Who do you want to emulate? What mistakes do you want to avoid?

Depending on your finances or where you are in your career, consider finding a personal stylist at a major department store. They will pick out clothes for you and help you develop your style. You won't save money but you will save time and you'll end up with great clothes that flatter you and build your confidence. You won't be wearing the same thing as everyone else. You'll also be left with fewer mistakes that linger unworn in your wardrobe.

Your appearance can strengthen your personal brand. Make sure the two are congruent and reinforcing each other.

Maximize Visibility

Emma worked at a global consumer products company. Recognized as a high performer, she had been rapidly promoted, but now, for some reason, was struggling. Her role involved working across teams and coordinating corporate efforts, but often without authority over the people she worked with. She found it hard to negotiate successfully, especially with more senior colleagues. Her boss, the global head of a corporate function, was tired of having to intervene and negotiate on her behalf. He told her she needed to improve her visibility and get more recognition for the initiatives she was leading. This, he argued, would give her more standing and make it easier for her to negotiate with others.

"Be more visible? What does that even mean? It's not like I'm wearing Harry Potter's cloak of invisibility. I am right here, doing my job," said Emma when we started working together.

Visibility can be particularly important in large companies, where you're working across matrices and your colleagues are spread across the country or the globe. Committees of senior colleagues who have never met you and have no stake in your success decide promotions and rewards. How do you make yourself more visible to them?

We could digress and have a conversation about how your work should speak for itself and your boss should be the one to lobby for you in those committees, but let's assume you already know that's not always the case.

WHY: Five reasons why you need to improve your visibility

1. You need to be more visible in order to be recognized and rewarded for the work you do.
2. If more senior colleagues are aware of the results you're getting, you are more likely to secure resources when you ask for them.
3. The people on your team ought to get credit for what they do, and you are the best person to get that for them.
4. Increasing your perceived value and marketability gives you better options to move, inside or outside the company.
5. Less talented people can do this well and if they get rewarded, you will resent it.

But how do you improve your visibility where you work? Pick an area of activity where there is corporate interest. This could be a corporate project, an employee affinity group, or an annual corporate event. Hint: Senior people will be involved. If they are not, stay away unless it's something you enjoy for its own sake.

HOW: Ways to rapidly increase your visibility

1. Volunteer, ask, or lobby to get involved. Offer to do a tedious job on a committee. Write about it for a staff newsletter. Make sure to attend any events or receptions related to this initiative. Show up early, network purposefully, and be aware that you are doing this deliberately to improve your visibility.

2. Offer to help out at senior-level retreats, even in an ancillary role. I know of one senior strategy officer, who was not part of the management team, but offered to take minutes at their offsite. The following year he was asked to facilitate their discussion. Not only was he sitting in on discussions of the senior team, to which even his own boss was not privy, but he was also able to build relationships and become well known to the people running the organization. He had unparalleled access, all

because he offered to do something as menial as typing.

3. Show up at corporate receptions and events. Arrive early when the hosts have to be present but most other staff haven't yet arrived. Senior people often don't know many people in the room and employees are reluctant to approach them.

4. The seat next to the CEO at the corporate picnic is often vacant. Take that spot. Be personable. Don't talk about work. Treat them like a colleague you don't know that well, ask questions, and share a little of your own life.

5. Hold an event to honor someone junior and invite their boss, or their boss's boss. The lower you go in the food chain of your organization, the easier this is to do and the more likely the senior person will turn out.

6. Write for corporate newsletters or your company's intranet site. The internal communications people are often desperate for content and out of ideas.

7. Invite a speaker to address employees at your company and invite someone senior to introduce them. Then write about it for the internal news outlet. You will find that you can get surprisingly high-level speakers for free if they are on a book tour and in the area.

Case Study: Having read a book that made a huge impression on her, Imani, a mid-level staffer at a large organization, organized a brown bag lunch with an employee affinity group to discuss the book. Interest was so high in the topic that she suggested inviting the author to their company to speak. The author came and the affinity group held a standing-room-only event open to all staff, at which Imami made the opening remarks. Knowing that not all the senior management would attend the session, she proposed a private lunch for the CEO and his team to meet with the author. The topic of the book was in an area declared important by the corporation. As the coordinator of the event, Imani made sure she was part of the group at the private lunch. She received serious amounts of visibility on an issue that management cared about and kudos for having the initiative to create an event from which all benefited.

Force yourself to talk to senior people in your company. They are often out of touch with the daily goings on and even lonely. They like to have other channels of information, apart from the senior executives that surround them, and they like to be seen as familiar with mid- and lower-ranking employees.

Ask them open-ended questions. Start a conversation as you would with any colleague you don't know well. Ask them about their involvement in the event you're both at, about their thinking on a current issue, or about their family life or career history. Offer your own views and experience. Tell them how this event relates to what you do, or suggest ways you'd like to get involved. Do your best, then go home.

To Boldly Go

You can have a lot of success in building your personal brand by being confident and courageous. Most importantly, it doesn't pay to care too much about what other people think.

In 1994, I was a junior reporter with Reuters news agency in Moscow. I met the agency's editor in chief there when he visited to open a new office. Editor in chief in a news agency is a big deal, a CEO equivalent. He said to stay in touch and have lunch when I was in London next. So I did. Several months later, I was reassigned to London. I called and set up a lunch appointment. When I told my then boss why I needed to be excused from my desk, his jaw dropped. I was a minion heading off to lunch with the big cheese.

I hadn't thought anything of it. Someone said look me up and we will have lunch, so I did. I didn't manage to leverage the occasion because I wasn't aware of what an opportunity it was and I failed to nurture the relationship. Ironically, if I had been more senior I probably would not have followed up, thinking that he invites everyone to lunch and doesn't mean it. I would have "overthought" the situation.

As our careers progress, we are often more reluctant to take people up on these kinds of offers. We fail to see opportunities to build our own brand and profile. We become timid and worry what others will think.

Here are seven easy ways to boldly build your brand.

1. **Find industry conferences and offer to speak.** Start small if you are junior. Look for angles. What are they missing from their typical lineup of panelists? Are they short on young people, women, or minorities? Are they missing new sectors or niche fields? Can you fill any of those gaps?

2. **Identify other speaking opportunities.** Get an assistant to scour the most important events in your industry and call the organizers to find out the lead-time for booking speakers. Put those dates on your calendar and call them.

3. **Write for industry newsletters and blogs.** Find out the rules at your company for doing that. If you need to, start small. Trade publications are often desperate for content. Being published regularly will make it more likely that you're invited to speak at events or asked to write for other outlets.

4. **Visit the pressroom at conferences, if there is one, and network.** Most people are too afraid to talk to reporters. That's crazy. If you know your subject matter and don't criticize others, you can safely become a reliable source for reporters covering your industry. This helps build your profile as well as that of your company.

5. **Invite experts to your company and host a brown bag lunch or equivalent.** The experts will be flattered. The cost is zero or very little. The result is you being seen as a connector to innovation and leaders in the outside world.

6. **Look for awards for which to nominate yourself or your team.** These are often low-hanging fruit. People don't actively look for these, leaving the organizers to revert to people they are already familiar with. They are often grateful for a fresh face. Search in trade publications and associations for relevant awards and mark the submission dates on your calendar.

7. **Think outside your industry.** If you are in the private sector, build relationships at international organizations like the United Nations or World Bank with a view to getting speaking opportunities at their events. People heading partnership functions like UN's Global Compact or external affairs are a good place

to start. Back at your own company, you will
be perceived as a global thought leader.

External validation is a great way to build your profile internally. But the key is to make sure the people who matter are aware of it.

Cultivate your internal communications function, if that exists at your company. Make it easy for them to cover the award you were shortlisted for (you don't have to win, think "Oscar nominee"). Or provide them with links to the articles you penned. If the articles mention your company, and they should, they can be included in the news round-up that most companies produce to distribute to staff and will be read by senior executives.

True Story: In one company where I worked, a particular senior manager was so adept at submitting events where she had spoken or articles she had written, that one day she was featured in two of the three top corporate news stories. A tally was done and it was discovered she had more placements and prominence over the course of the previous three months in internal news channels than the CEO— all because she had submitted items of interest and they had been accepted. Needless to say, the internal communications team got their knuckles rapped for being so easily manipulated. No blame fell to her.

Having done all of that and been confident and coura-geous about building your personal brand, the next step is to boldly go further. Why not go for that senior position or promotion? Or leave the company you're with to join a new one? The longer you stay in one organization, the harder it becomes to leave. But once you've made a change, your ability to change again increases dramatically. The logic of that is that if things don't work out, it will be easier than you currently think to move on.

If, after reading Chapter 1, you've identified the type of life you'd like to create, does your current job support that? Are you happy doing what you're doing?

For some people, the current job supports other goals they have and even if it's not very satisfying, the other goals are so important as to outweigh any unhappiness.

But if that's not the case for you and you regularly complain to friends about how cheesed off you are, then you need to consider making a change, or you will never live the life you want.

Got Gravitas? (aka Presence)

I have worked with executive coaching clients who have been told they need to acquire more gravitas. But what does that mean, and how do you acquire some?

Gravitas is defined as "dignity, seriousness, or solem-nity of manner or bearing." Leaving aside the merits of that and what may lie in the eye of the beholder, the following exercise includes suggestions for some instant gravitas.

Exercise: *Make eye contact with your interlocutor, keep your feet flat on the ground, and hold your body nice and steady. Listen carefully to what they're saying. Repeat back what they said, checking for understanding. Confirm understanding. Pause. Now ask an open question to explore their point of view. It's basically active listening, while paying attention to your body language. It's not all you can do to develop gravitas, but it's a very good place to start. Try it.*

But gravitas can't be achieved just by active listening. It's part of the larger issue of "presence." Presence is another trait that many of you have been told you need to develop. Or maybe you've been told you need to adapt your presence for your audience.

The key to developing a positive presence is having more awareness of your impact. Your impact is how others experience you, regardless of what you intended. It's how what you said or did landed with them. It varies by person and circumstance.

Have you ever been told you were "shouting" at someone, when you clearly weren't shouting? That's impact.

The other person experienced your tone and body language as "shouting." It happens a lot with teenagers but also with colleagues who are of a much quieter disposition than you or who are much subordinate to you.

Intent vs. Impact

There is often a gap between intent and impact. Only the person on the receiving end can know what impact you had on them, and only you can know your intent.

It seems obvious, but think about it for a minute. If that's the case, you will never know what impact you had unless they tell you or you ask. Likewise, they won't know what you intended, unless you say.

The lesson here is to check assumptions and signpost for your listener. If you tell people what you intend, you're making it easier for them to experience you as you intended.

> **Example #1:** "I'm going to go through the timeline for this project, as I see it, and then get your feedback, okay?"
>
> **Not:** "We need to get proposals in by June, select a provider by July, and have first-round drafts by August...."

> **Example #2:** "I'd like to give you some feedback on your presentation because you've said you are working on your public speaking skills. Would you like that?"

Not: "I thought your presentation was decent, but you could have done a better job explaining the data."

Ceilings and Floors

People have different tolerances for behavior. For some listeners, when you speak quickly with energy and gestures, it conveys enthusiasm and invigorates. For others, the same behavior is overwhelming and domineering. Think of this as ceilings and floors. The limit of my tolerance for your energy is my ceiling, but that may be someone else's floor, because they love high energy. Figuring out the ceilings and floors of your audience is critical.

Case Study: Michael was a senior executive in a European media company. He thrived in the fast-paced environment and was known for being a creative thinker who continually disrupted and innovated. Some of the company's newest products and revenue lines came from his group. He was loud and brash and funny. His team loved him. They were young and creative, working in the digital space where boundaries were broken every day.

As a member of the senior team, Michael had to present on occasion to Ted, the CEO. Ted was an

---

> *analytical introvert. Michael's normal level of energy grated on him. Ted had said he found Michael scattered and confusing. In order to bring his intent and impact closer, Michael practiced presenting for Ted with restraint. He was more thoughtful about which points he needed to make and making them succinctly. "Speak less, smile more," became his mantra in the room with Ted. That helped him listen more effectively and contribute more salient points.*

As you think more about your presence and impact, take a look around and look for examples of people whose impact is probably not what they intended. You'll see it in the spoken and written word, as well as in body language.

Focus on the Physical

Physical body language is often the one thing we forget as the speaker, but its impact on a listener can be profound. This is especially the case when our body language is at odds with our spoken or written word.

A colleague once accused me of rolling my eyes every time she spoke up in a meeting. It's true I thought her ideas were lousy, but I had no idea I was "leaking" my opinion so obviously and so unkindly.

An example of body language trumping the spoken and written word was apparent in March 2015 when the

CEOs of Lufthansa and German Wings came together in public after a German Wings pilot had deliberately crashed a plane in the Alps, killing all 150 people on board. Lufthansa owned the low-cost carrier German Wings and repeatedly stated that they were a united executive team and had full confidence in each other. However, it was apparent from their body language at a press conference that the two men were at odds and barely knew one another.

Think about cultivating a presence that reinforces your personal brand. If you want to be considered an effective, trustworthy, senior player in the organization, start acting that way. Think about your impact on others and tailoring your style for your audience. Check out how others experience you. Is it in line with your intent? Is it in line with your personal brand? Is in line with your values?

Act the Part

A former colleague of mine, Jo, based in Hong Kong with a large financial institution, got a call one day from an executive he knew in mainland China. They had previously met at an industry conference. The executive was calling because he was applying for a job at Jo's company and wanted some insight about the role and the organization. Jo assumed he was interested in a recently advertised investment role in the region. The executive was actually applying to be CEO of the corporation. He got the job.

Jo wasn't off base in assuming the executive meant the lesser role. The executive had never worked outside China and was not a global partner in his firm. He was a regional leader within China for a large investment firm.

The recruiters never really figured that out. They assumed he was a global partner and responsible for the entire country. The executive never lied. He thought he could do the job and acted accordingly. It was only when the press release announcing his appointment was rejected by his former employer, that it became apparent he had been a regional VP, not a corporate partner. By then it was too late; there had been endless rounds of interviews and confirmation by the board of directors. The press release was amended to be pleasantly vague and the new CEO began his tenure.

Sometimes you have to act the part before you have it. You can call it "fake it until you make it," but there's more to it than that.

Acting the part means being the person you want to be. It means behaving as though you are already in the more senior role. It means looking for opportunities to be with the people you want as your peers.

There are plenty of ways to do this. Some of them are outlined earlier in the chapter, in opportunities to be visible and raise your profile.

There is also what you need to stop doing. If you aspire to be taken more seriously, you need to stop identifying so closely with people who complain and indulge in conspiracy theories around the water cooler. You generally won't find senior colleagues there, at least not successful ones. So quit that scene and find another.

Growing Up in the Organization

One of the challenges of being in an organization for any length of time is that people are used to seeing you in a certain light. This can be particularly problematic for women who are often less adept or less willing to self-promote and network. The phenomenon of "growing up in an organization" is that both you and your colleagues still see you in your initial junior role. You're still there in your head and they forget you've been promoted since you arrived.

You're the one who needs to change. Your colleagues won't and they might not like it when you do. This is a little like family dynamics, when you try to act around your family as the person you are with your friends, and your family members emotionally bludgeon you back into your traditional role as the baby, the under-achiever, or whatever stereotype they find more comfortable.

That's why you have to act the part, in life as well as at the office. You have to behave the way you want to be, the way you want to live and work. You can't wait for others to grant you that role or give you a title. You simply have to assume it and keep going until they get used to the new you.

Sometimes it's easier to start with small things—speaking up more often in meetings or not offering to do something menial. The physical aspect is important, and dressing for success can help mask your anxiety and give you greater confidence. If you know you look good, you generally also feel good. That makes it easier to try new behaviors.

No Prophet Is Accepted in His Hometown

One easy way to act the part is not to be known. It's much easier to start behaving differently when people don't know how you were before. Think of people who move out of a company or town and talk about the freedom they had to reinvent themselves and lose some of the traits and history that held them back.

The bible verse phrase, "No prophet is accepted in his own country," in the Gospel of Luke 4:24, comes to mind. It is often easier to influence or impress strangers than those who have known you for years. Starting over with a clean slate can be a huge advantage.

That's why some of the anxiety people have about switching companies or career tracks is often misguided. You get a bump for being new and unknown. Hemingway talked about the attraction of the "new and strange" in *A Moveable Feast*.[1] The principle applies in the workplace as well as in Paris.

If starting over with a clean slate is not an option, you can still begin acting the part and slowly wean yourself, and those around you, off the old you. Then both you and they will start to see you the way you want to be.

At home it can help to signal the changes you're making and ask the people who love you for their support. If you want more time for pleasure and want your partner or spouse to join you, it helps to explain to them why it's important to you and how you think it will also benefit them. That generally goes down better than proposing a date night out of the blue and being irritated at all the reasons they give for why Thursday won't work.

Engagement Creates Momentum

I often work with coaching clients who are looking for new roles. In some cases, they are looking within their current companies. In others, they have left and are seeking new opportunities. The singular hallmark of those who do well is what I call "engagement."

Engagement describes those who actively reach out to others, set up meetings and informational coffees, and go to events and conferences. When they do this, they meet other people, have further conversations, and get new ideas and connections to pursue. They place more calls, read up, and do more research. Then the dots start to connect, the path forward becomes a little clearer, and some paths are ruled out.

Sometimes it's hard. Calls or emails aren't returned. People don't respond with enthusiasm. But my most successful clients keep at it. The more engaged they are, the more momentum they create, and that momentum results in decisions and great offers for new roles.

The same applies to building a strong personal brand and creating the career and life you want. Acting the part is really about living the part. It's about purposefully doing the things you want, and behaving as you want to be. By persisting, you will create momentum that becomes self-reinforcing and, ultimately, self-sustaining.

8

The Power of Pleasure

*I*n a nutshell: In the 19th century, the upper classes didn't tend to work much. As the dowager countess on Downton Abbey *asked:* "What's a weekend?"[1] It was assumed that increased productivity would mean more leisure. Instead, being busy became a status symbol. Now that's starting to change, and having control over one's life and time is the new sign of success.

Pleasure and Leisure

Bertrand Russell, the British philosopher, wrote an essay "In Praise of Idleness," published in 1935. In it, he laid out his thinking on work and the importance of leisure.[2] He saw the Industrial Revolution as a way to reduce the amount of time workers spent laboring and believed that the ultimate goal of technological advancement was to increase the amount of leisure available to the average person.

> Bertrand Russell's central argument is that work is not the purpose of life and that we overvalue it.

Russell espoused a four-hour workday. If automation allowed us to accomplish more in less time, we should use the remaining time for pleasure and for good, not for more work.

He argued that civilization had been the fruit of having an elite, leisure class. He acknowledged that the elite had enjoyed advantages unfairly and their leisure had been earned on the backs of oppressed laborers, serfs, and slaves throughout the centuries. However, he made the case that the same elite had been responsible for much of what was good in the civilized world. Without an elite that had the leisure to pursue their interests, we wouldn't have the art, science, literature, and even the philosophical or political thought that created the great civilizations.

In Russell's worldview, industrialization now made it possible for everyone to enjoy the same benefits. He was no romantic when it came to the merits of the ruling classes and caustic in his judgment. He felt that the vast majority of the ruling classes were indolent and lacking in talent. Although the upper classes had produced Darwin and many other great minds, most of its members were more concerned with the state of their horses and their next meal or entertainment.

Russell believed that much good would come from people having more leisure—not only would they have personal satisfaction, but society as a whole would benefit. He thought that a small minority of people, if given the freedom to explore their interests unrelated to their employment, would pursue interests that contributed to the common good. They would engage in causes and movements that made life better for everyone. They would seek to improve how things are done, which would benefit all.

His main concern, however, was for the quality of life of the individual. He wanted people to be healthy and happy, to live calm lives engaged with each other. His ideal was that work would be demanding enough to make leisure appreciated, but not so much that it left people exhausted and unable for anything else.

Yet, we don't seem to take advantage of it as we should:

"Modern methods of production have given us the possibility of ease and security for all; we have chosen, instead, to have overwork for some and starvation for others. Hitherto we have continued to be as energetic as we were before there were machines; in this we have been foolish, but there is no reason to go on being foolish forever."[3]

Russell was writing in the 1930s. He was already seeing that the Industrial Revolution had not resulted in a reduction of work as he thought it should. If he were alive now, he would see that we continue to be as "foolish" as ever and show no signs of changing our ways.

People now wear "busyness" as a badge of honor and sign of importance. Long-hours cultures are rife across many industries, notably in law and financial services. In the United States, vacation for most employees is set at two weeks a year and even that holiday leave is not always taken.

The headlines capture the extreme cases, like the banking intern in London who died of epileptic shock after working 72 hours in a row or junior doctors who regularly work back-to-back overnight shifts.

But what about the rest of us? To what end is all this work?

Dolce Far Niente

dol·ce far nien·te \ dōlCHā ˌfär nēˈentā—An Italian phrase that translates as "pleasant idleness" or "the pleasure of doing nothing."

The Italians feel very strongly about *dolce far niente*. For them it means idling away an hour in a café with friends or pottering solo along city streets with no particular destination in mind. You can *dolce far niente* alone or with someone. It doesn't mean hanging out or just doing nothing. There's a sweetness or wistfulness to it that implies you are appreciating the moment and have chosen to do nothing on purpose, for the pleasure of it. There is a sense of gentle idleness about it.

Americans don't really do *dolce far niente*. Life is to be conquered and squeezed to the fullest. If you have down time, it should be optimized, utilized, prioritized. Think of all the things you could be doing in this hour or two. The idea of enjoying doing nothing feels heretical, sinful, and shameful.

I have a good friend who worries about wasting time. She will often end a sentence about what her family ought to be doing with the phrase, "So the day isn't wasted." This was particularly amusing on a ski trip we were taking together with three preteen boys. The boys were sleeping in, lounging around in their pajamas, and slowly eating a pancake breakfast while she fretted that if they didn't get moving and onto the slopes, the day would be wasted. It's hard not to see the irony in hurrying along someone who is obviously enjoying themselves to enjoy themselves better doing something else.

I have a lot of sympathy for my friend. I like the satisfaction of getting things done and the sense of achievement that comes in ticking off a to-do list. The problem is that the items on the list are self-replacing. You've never ticked anything off without adding more items. And meanwhile, the moment for relaxing has passed.

Here are some suggestions for how you can enjoy *dolce far niente*. You will probably have plenty of others to add to this list, but it's a good start:

- **Unplug**—Take a two-hour sabbatical from your devices. Don't check email or calls while doing something pleasant.
- **Get out doors**—The next time the sun is shining, get up from your desk and take a 30-minute walk outside. Look around you and see what you notice that you've never seen before.
- **Coffee with yourself**—Instead of carrying your coffee back to your desk, sit and drink it without doing anything else (no phone, no newspaper). Look around you; lose yourself in your own thoughts.
- **Leave early**—Leave your office earlier than usual and wander back home taking an unusual route or stopping off at a bookstore to browse.
- **Mooch**—On Saturday morning, don't head off straight away to the gym or to run errands. Stay in your pajamas, drink coffee and call a friend.
- **Be early**—Next time you're meeting someone for dinner, try to be half an hour early and have a drink at the bar, people-watching until your companions arrive.
- **Sabbatical Sunday (or Saturday)**—You don't have to be religious to take a Sabbath day. Decide which of your two weekend days will be errand-free. Do the necessary errands on the other day and only plan fun, pleasurable activities on your "Sabbath."

Leader Profile: Caroline Kende Robb

When I spoke with Caroline Kende Robb, executive director of the Africa Progress Panel, she was at pains to make it clear that she wasn't comfortable being singled out as an example of a successful leader.

"I am always very reluctant to say I've been successful here or I've been successful there, because you don't know what's going to happen going forward. So far, I've managed to balance my work and my life, and so far the outcome is quite balanced. It's that "so far" because you don't know what kind of challenges you might face or what might happen in the future," she said.

But "so far" she has done a very good job of having a dynamic career and rich personal life. She began her career with Marks & Spencer, the British retailer, and went on to a distinguished career in the UK government, World Bank, and IMF, where she was a pioneer in the field of social policy and development in poor countries. Five years ago, Kofi Annan, former head of the United Nations, tapped her to run the Africa Progress Panel, an organization he chairs that seeks behind-the-scenes solutions to the most intractable problems on the continent.

"In terms of my career, ever since I was about 9, I had a sense of social injustice and all I ever wanted to do was the work that I'm involved in now. That's always been quite clear. I've not struggled with thinking what do I want to do with my life. I've seen my job more as a vocation than a job."

Caroline has three young children and is married to a successful consultant in the telecoms industry. They currently live in Geneva.

Caroline attributes her success to being focused on productivity. She describes being "super focused" when at work and constantly making trade-offs on choosing to do the things that will have the most impact and ditching the ones with the least impact. "Influencing policy in countries has a huge long-term impact. That's an area my time is well spent," she said.

"I work very hard and leave on time. I am very organized during the day and don't get distracted. I think I am good at self-reflection. I always ask what could I have done better. I am also good at asking for help. I look for experts, ask friends. I like to bounce ideas around with my team."

In terms of her personal life, it revolves around family and spending time with her girls and friends and family. "I like having rituals of things we do together, whether that's cooking together, eating together, their individual bedtime routines. The routine things, like our breakfast and dinner together, those are the most important things to me."

The Luxury of Time

There is a counter-movement starting to emerge of people bragging about how they don't check their email on vacation or about the unusual and lengthy holidays they've been taking. I know one executive whose most recent holidays included kayaking above the Arctic Circle in Norway and floating down a river in a barge in India.

Lucy Kellway at the *Financial Times* has been documenting how bankers in London are now as likely to brag about their New Year's resolutions of cutting down on long hours as they are about cutting down on alcohol.[4]

There is a slow-dawning recognition that being truly successful means having control over your diary. If you were top of your game, why would you be at the beck and call of clients and corporate schedules?

Some sectors are slower to adapt to this phenomenon than others. Lawyers are notorious for working long hours because their business model is based on number of hours billed rather than on value provided. (Slight digression here, but how logical is it to charge more for taking longer to do something?)

I know a very successful international lawyer who is considered the leading expert in his field, but he laments the amount of time he spends traveling, including back and forth to Asia twice a month, and the conference calls that go past midnight.

"The clients demand it," he will say. "I really don't have that much control."

How is that much different from the factory workers who slaved 12 hours a day, six days a week to whom
Bertrand Russell wanted to provide more leisure time?

My lawyer friend literally has about as much leisure
time as a 19th-century coal worker! He lives in much
greater comfort, of course, and drives a very nice car, but
the level of control he has over his life and how he spends
his time is about as limited.

The television series *Downton Abbey* portrayed the
last glorious days of the British upper classes when life was
predestined from birth and some were born to serve and
others to be served. The period captured in the award-
winning drama is the early 20th century—the decades
before World War II and the ensuing social leveling that
would come in the post-war period due to advances in
automation, access to education, and the need for a more
skilled workforce.

The inhabitants of Downton Abbey spent their days
engaged in leisurely pursuits and some amount of good
works. The Dowager Countess once asked quite genuinely
of her relative Matthew, who worked for a living as a solic-
itor, "What's a weekend?"

The pendulum has come full circle where most people
now long for more leisure and the very successful actually
have less of it than others.

This is where I think the change is taking place
and people are starting to push back and challenge

conventional wisdom. What is the purpose of my life? Is it to struggle up the corporate ladder in order to toil there like an indentured servant? How is that success?

I've worked with many executives, women in particular, who look at the senior people in their organizations—both male and female—and decide that's not what they want.

"I was encouraged to apply for a director role. It's considered very prestigious. But when I looked at the current directors and saw how much time they spend at work and how much time they spend traveling, I decided I really didn't want to live like that. I feel bad because I know I should try to advance my career, but that just doesn't look attractive," said a mid-level executive at a global financial institution.

If time is the ultimate luxury, what implication does that have for employers?

"I would much rather have every Friday off and forgo 20 percent of my pay than have to go to work five days a week," said a senior female executive in the UK. "That one extra day makes a huge difference to my life and time with my family. Even though I check email on Fridays and am probably as productive as someone else doing five days, I like the freedom it gives me."

If you're an employer or leader in your organization, figuring out what people really value at work is crucial to your success. Hint: It's not more money.

Experiences vs. Consumption

I once took a trip to Nicaragua with my son over spring break. It was a bit of a disaster. We stayed in what had appeared to be idyllic beach bungalows on a remote island. But the sea was too rough for swimming, there was no pool, the nearest restaurant was a 20-minute walk on a muddy path through the jungle, and the resort owners were mean and rude. We tried to leave but couldn't get a flight out earlier than the one on which we were booked. "We are trapped in paradise, Mom," said my then 13-year-old son.

We made the best of things, got ourselves qualified in scuba diving, and were grateful for our Kindles. We now retell stories from the trip with much hilarity, including how the resort owners refused to serve us lunch one day because we hadn't booked ahead even though we were staying there all week, and how they hid the fresh milk saying they needed it to make cheese and couldn't spare it for guests.

The same thing doesn't happen when I buy something or order it online and it turns out to be the wrong size or not as it appeared. There's nothing hilarious in that. I simply have the tedium of repacking and shipping it back to the seller.

What's the difference? A lot, apparently.

There has been significant research done into the difference in pleasure we get from experiences versus things. Research led by Cornell psychology professor Thomas

Gilovich found that "Experiential purchases (money spent on *doing*) tend to provide more enduring happiness than material purchases (money spent on *having*)."[5]

Extensive research by Gilovich and colleagues found that there was a reason my nightmare trip to Nicaragua still gave me more pleasure than a purchase, satisfactory or not.

Apparently the benefits of experiences start to accrue in advance of the actual experience and have an afterlife in our memory. The same is not true of purchases.

"You can think about waiting for a delicious meal at a nice restaurant or looking forward to a vacation," one of the researchers on Gilovich's team said, "and how different that feels from waiting for, say, your pre-ordered iPhone to arrive. Or when the two-day shipping on Amazon Prime doesn't seem fast enough."[6]

We get more pleasure thinking about the pleasure we are going to have from an experience in the future, something we don't get when we think about possessions.

You would think we would enjoy our new sofa more than our weekend away because it's permanent and we derive ongoing enjoyment from it. Not true. It seems we have infinite capacity to become bored or unappreciative of the object for the very fact that we see it every day. Just think how quickly your euphoria at your new iPhone dissipated as it simply became your phone.

It turns out we also enjoy waiting for an experience much more than waiting for a possession.[7] Witness the mood and interactions between people lined up to see the latest *Star Wars* movie or attend a concert of their favorite band, and compare it to the lack of mirth among sales shoppers on Good Friday or New Year's Eve.

For retailers, our preference for experiences has major ramifications. A recent study by Ernst & Young found that the number-one trend among consumers was what they termed "prioritization of experiential value."[8] What that translates into is that it's not enough that you sell me that coat and that it keeps me warm; I want to enjoy the experience of buying it and have a connection with the brand. Consumers are now expecting to be "active co-creators instead of simply consumers." Retailers are now encouraging customers to participate at various stages, from design to purchase. They are also trying to add more experience by creating platforms for customers to have community with each other.

Next time you have a tech question, notice how the company you're dealing with will steer you toward a "user forum," where you can ask other customers how best to resolve whatever issue you're facing. This saves the company money on customer service and you're likely to feel happier because you're connecting with other like-minded, but hopefully more adept, customers.

This sort of consumer interaction hosted by a retailer lends itself to areas like tech, but it is increasingly found for everything from coffee to home appliance purchases.

The chief lesson here is that experiences make us happier than possessions and the likely conclusion is that the longer we spend anticipating them, the more pleasure we get. So try less impulse buying and fewer surprise parties, and instead start planning that next vacation.

The Natural World

Only 15 percent of Americans today live in rural areas, a phenomenon shared with most industrialized countries. We love cities for their conveniences and the economies of scale they produce. Cities are responsible for much of what civilization has to offer. Without cities, ideas can't spread and people can't develop and produce things for others as easily. It's hard to provide services to people settled in remote areas, located long distances from each other. All manner of human endeavor and community do better in cities, whether that's schools and hospitals, or orchestras and coffee shops. And yet, city living can be tiring and wearying. The noise, building height, traffic, congestion, and crowds all take a toll on our collective psyches.

Research on the impact of urban life is well established. Living in an urban environment is long known to be a risk factor for psychiatric diseases such as major depression or schizophrenia. This is true even though infrastructure, socioeconomic conditions, nutrition, and health care services are better in cities than in rural areas.[9]

But what about the benefits of nature to mitigate the stress of urban life, either within an urban environment or by spending time in rural settings?

It seems that although this research is less well established, we benefit substantially from spending time in nature.

Research by Gregory Bratman at Stanford University investigated the impact of nature experience on affect and cognition.[10] Bratman and his colleagues randomly assigned 60 participants to a 50-minute walk in either a natural or an urban environment in and around Stanford, California. Before and after their walk, participants completed a series of psychological assessments of affective and cognitive functioning.

Compared to the urban walk, the nature walk resulted in affective benefits (decreased anxiety, rumination, and negative affect, and preservation of positive affect) as well as cognitive benefits (increased working memory performance).

In other words, the same walk had more benefit if it took place in nature. Perhaps it's hardly surprising that a walk along the highway would be more stressful than a walk alongside a pretty stream, but an interesting aspect of the research was the benefit that continued after the walk was over.

Those participants who had walked along the highway were more likely to ruminate on things that were troubling them and report feeling anxious, while the participants who had been on a ramble through greenery reported feeling more confident, happy, and optimistic about their lives. The natural environment was the better one for participants' brains.

The research on the impact of water to calm our nervous systems and increase well-being is even more compelling. Why are people drawn to spend time beside water in the summer, whether that's the seashore or a lake? And why do people like to retire beside water? It may seem self-evident that we acquire mental benefits from being near water, but it turns out those benefits are far greater than we may have imagined.

Marine biologist Wallace J. Nichols has done extensive research on the remarkable effects of water on our health and well-being. In his book *Blue Mind*, he explores the neuroscience behind the benefits of being in, on, under, or beside water.[11]

Nichols shares stories from top athletes, scientists, military veterans, and artists to show how water can improve performance, increase calm, diminish anxiety, and increase professional success. Fortunately, we don't have to live beside the sea to benefit; swimming in our local pool or taking a bath has similar benefits to spending time by the ocean.

The benefits of being closer to nature may not seem like much of a revelation. For decades there have been organizations that worked to bring inner-city children to the country.

Summer camps dot the country now, but they started initially in the North East as a way to get children out of the heat and congestion of industrialized cities out to the country. To this day, camps compete with each other to draw urban children and their parents based on their proximity to water and distance from towns. Often, the more remote the camp, the more expensive it is.

Although we know it intuitively, spending time in nature is restorative and rejuvenating in ways we are still only beginning to appreciate.

In the meantime, experiment on yourself and notice the difference between a walk on a treadmill and one in the woods.

9

Long-Term Goals

I *n a nutshell: Long-term planning is hard in the throes of working full time, especially alongside the demands of family. But if you don't put some key pieces in place, you run the risk of someday asking what it was all for. Later, as you get to the highest point in your corporate life, you need to start figuring out the transition to the next stage, to a portfolio life of professional, personal, and philanthropic pursuits.*

The Wake-Up Call

How many of us have marveled as we listened to distinguished colleagues or speakers talk about how they planned their career? You've listened to them reflecting on how one thing built on the other, from college, to graduate school, to their first job, and then on in a seemingly seamless progression.

For most of us, it doesn't go like that. I remember listening with some frustration to Colin Powell, retired four-star general and former Secretary of State, an incredibly accomplished individual and powerful speaker, urging his audience to take the advice that had served him so well: "Always be looking for that which you do well and that which you love doing, and when you find those two things together, man, you got it."[1]

If only it were that easy. Most of us do not find that what we do well is also something we love easily or early. Some never find it at all. And for others, it changes over time.

However, it's a good maxim to reflect on, to see how close we are to achieving that goal or how far away from it we stand. If you hate what you do and are only average at it, then you really need to take a look at what you're doing with your life.

Some people get a wake-up call, like a health scare or a rupture in a relationship, which causes them to reassess what they're doing with their lives. But most of us don't. Most of us move along from one year to the next, from one job to the next, making choices as we go, but not seeing a pattern and not consciously laying out a path with a destination.

Until we look in the rearview mirror and see how it all unfolded, the impact of some of the choices we make seems small at the time.

I had a colleague at the United Nations in New York who used to talk about a tactical error he thought he had made in staying too long in a particular organization, but had later concluded it was a strategic error because the role had locked him into an entire career path with limited options for exiting. The magnitude of the decision to stay became increasingly amplified as the years passed and was something he regretted.

It's a cliché to say that no one regrets not spending enough time in the office on his or her deathbed. But some fascinating reports from older people, gathered by David Brooks of the *New York Times*, compiles what makes for the happiest of lives.

One of the key findings was of the benefit of dividing life into chapters, however artificial that seems. Those who did so reported feeling they had had more control over their lives and the direction they took, than those who felt they had bobbed along on an "unbroken flow like a cork."[2]

Other key lessons included to be wary of ruminating, rather move onward and upward; don't try to control others, because you can't and it will frustrate you; and take more risk rather than less. Older people generally regretted more the things they hadn't done, rather than the things they had done. That coincides with Dan Gilbert's research on decision-making.[3] The seniors also wrote about the pleasures of positive relationships and being a member of communities, as well as working inside organizations and crafts, rather than staying outside as rebels or lone wolves.

Dozens of older people's life stories are gathered on Brooks's blog and make for fascinating reading, at times harrowing and melancholy, often funny and touching.

Reading them may be enough to give you space to reflect on what you'd like to write as your life story. To help you do that, try this exercise:

Exercise: *Write a letter to yourself five years from now. Write about what you're currently doing, how your life is, what you value, and what you dislike about it. Write to yourself about what you hope to be doing in five years' time and what you hope will have occurred in the time that elapses between then and now. If five years feels too long, then write a letter for a year out. When you're done, seal the envelope, address it to yourself, and put the date on which it is to be opened. Place it somewhere safe, with important personal documents or inside a journal, where you'll remember its location.*

This is your own wake-up call. You don't have to wait until you're 70 to decide if this was the direction in which you'd like to take your life. You can do it right now.

Financial Prudence, Personal Abundance

One of the biggest mistakes people make when planning for the long term financially is being overly optimistic. We always assume we will earn more in the future and never less. Our mental trajectory is a series of salary increases and bigger jobs or a growing business. This is generally true, but definitely not a given. Circumstances change, economies and industries decline, and health issues and personal obligations intervene.

A woman I know, having attended Princeton for her undergraduate degree and law school, began her career as a public defender, a demanding but intellectually rewarding career defending low-income clients in the judicial system. She assumed she would continue in this field for some time. Then her second child was born with special needs and she found herself needing to cut back and work part-time in order to care for him. Her career has continued to be extremely rewarding; she now primarily works on death penalty cases, but her earning power has certainly been impacted and she couldn't sustain her lifestyle without the second income provided by her husband.

Policymakers have long known about people's unrealistic optimism about the future. It's the same tendency that causes us not to contribute as much as we should to pension plans, to put off saving for a rainy day, and to assume the value of our homes will increase every year.

Behavioral economics is the field of study about the psychological and emotional factors of how we make decisions. More and more it is used by policymakers to make it easier for us to make decisions that are good for us, like contributing to our pension, and making it harder for us to do things that harm us, like smoking.

A useful primer in behavioral economics, as well as a fascinating read, is the book *Nudge* by Richard Thaler and Cass Sunstein, which collected examples of how governments could "nudge" people toward making better decisions.[4]

In the United Kingdom, a "Nudge unit" was set up within the Prime Minister's office to create policies that "enable people to make better choices for themselves." The unit also aimed to improve public services and make them easier to use, drawing on ideas from behavioral science literature. It was the world's first government institution dedicated to the application of behavioral sciences and has since been spun off as an independent entity that operates globally.

You can create your own nudge unit by assessing which areas of your personal finances could do with decision-making that is focused on the long term.

You might want to consult a reputable financial advisor, one with fiduciary responsibility, to help you map out your long-term financial goals. Focus on the building blocks of appropriate levels and types of insurance for when things don't work out as planned: health, life, home, disability, and so on. Then move to the planning for the future: retirement account, home ownership, college tuition for children, and the like. Set up automatic increases to pension and savings contributions. You won't miss what you never had.

As you put little "nudges" in place, don't think that means you're putting on a hair shirt. You're simply building structures that make it easier for you to get the big things right. You can still have plenty of personal abundance in your life. Abundance is a mindset, not a specific amount of money. Abundance is knowing you've made the right decisions in the long-term plan and you can enjoy the pleasures of life in the present.

Personal abundance is about being happy with your choices and decisions and not looking at others for validation. Abundance is not impulsive spendthrift behavior. Abundance is knowing when you can treat yourself and when you would rather stick to your plan knowing the long-term benefits that it will accrue.

If You Plan It, They Will Come

"I'll need at least five bedrooms, and it has to be lakeside."

The senior executive who told me this was single, recently divorced, and the property he was looking at was a 10-hour drive from where he lived. "Why's that?" I asked.

"Because if it's not lakeside, they won't come in summer and if there aren't enough bedrooms, they won't be able to bring their kids."

The people he was talking about were 15, 13, and 10 years old at the time, but he was planning ahead.

My friend was thinking about when his children would be grown and how he could ensure he would get to spend time with them. He wanted to make a plan that would maximize the chances of them wanting to spend time with him.

He wanted to make it easy and inviting for them, so they would factor in a couple of weeks' vacation a year at a family place, a place where they would see their siblings, and where they could bring their friends and, eventually, their own families.

And he wanted to get a start on that now, even though he would not be able to spend much time there initially. He had a demanding job and traveled a great deal. Custody of the children was split with his ex-wife, so there was only every alternate spring break, and other holidays, and the kids went to summer camps for large parts of the summer.

Yet there he was, poring over maps and real estate listings, looking for the perfect family compound. He was searching for something that would work now but that they could also grow into.

I thought this was a better approach than one taken by the CEO of a global media company. This was someone who was listed in the top 15 highest-paid CEOs in the United States. He had been telling colleagues his plans for Christmas and New Year's, which included flying his extended family by private jet first to Paris for a week and then on to Madagascar. He said family holidays had become more and more elaborate as he tried to keep the interest of his grown children by offering once-in-a-lifetime trips that only he could afford to provide.

By comparison, my friend looking at dilapidated farm-houses on lakes in New England is probably on to something better, in my view. By making the holiday home available to others to create their own trips and memories, he is extending the parameters for meaningful memories.

We know that experiences give us more pleasure and create more happiness than things. But experiences generally need to be planned for. It's hard to impulse-buy a family vacation.

If that's the case, and we are thinking in the long term about the life we want with the people we love, then planning to ensure those experiences happen becomes really important.

Great Memories, With a Little Planning

Here's a quick way to ensure you're taking time to create memories with the people you love:

- Take out your calendar and look at the next 12 months. It's easier to do this with a paper calendar than electronic (just saying).
- Now mark the high holidays, federal holidays, and any vacation already planned.

- Mark the places where you would like to take any additional time off, but haven't planned anything yet. Summer next year, for example.
- Look for gaps or long stretches where there are no holidays. Put an asterisk there. Can you take a break there? If not, those are great times to get theater tickets or plan a special dinner.

If you live with others, share the plan as a draft and get some input. Where would they like to go? What would they like to do? Then start putting some of the planning steps in place, making reservations, asking others to join you, and so on.

If you don't plan it, it's hard for others to join you. You also lose out on the benefits of anticipation, which we previously discussed. Remember: Half the pleasure of the trip is thinking about it beforehand.

A group of my girlfriends used to plan a small ski trip every January over Martin Luther King weekend. We would go to a local ski resort, a two- to three-hour drive at most, no flights or airlines. We would rent a house on a nearby lake, as large or small as the group needed, and pile in. Families would take turns cooking in the evening, and we fixed breakfast for children and ourselves. Lunch was on the mountain. Evenings were for board games, movies, and too much time in the hot tub. It was great fun, inexpensive, easily organized, and always very memorable. Eventually the children outgrew the resort and each other, but we still reminisce about some of the more hilarious moments: the child who wanted to move to the rental because it was nicer than his real home, the father who thought his children weren't far enough out on the ice, and the couple who insisted we all roll in the snow after being in the hot tub.

The memories you create also need a place to live on, beyond when you get together to recall what happened. That's easier than ever now. Take plenty of photos but make sure to upload them and turn them into photo-books, slideshows, or calendars. You can hit "auto fill" and still end up with something special. They also make a great gift for the host or friends who joined you. Now you are guaranteeing a long-lasting benefit from those moments.

Professional Legacy

A colleague, who retired after 30 years at the same insti-tution, was beloved. He had worked in many parts of the organization and held the number-two position, effec-tively COO, at the end of his career. He had even been acting CEO for the final few months before he left. There had been some talk of him possibly getting the top job, but he didn't. Instead that role went to an outsider, found by recruiters and vetted by the board. Whether he had even wanted the top role was uncertain, but he likely had.

At his leaving reception, amid the funny anecdotes and remembrances of some crazy trips to crazy clients in the "old days," much of the talk was of the fact that he was going to be replaced by two people. His job was effectively being divided into two, and two people would split the portfolio of responsibilities that he alone had managed.

The conversation was not one of wonder and admiration that it would take two people to fill his shoes, but rather that it was hardly surprising that no one would want his job, at least not all of it.

My colleague had been famous for being completely devoted to his work to the exclusion of all else. He was there early in the morning and late at night, at every committee meeting and board meeting. He knew the details of every major transaction that was ever undertaken, and although he took vacation in the summer, he could always be reached by email, no matter the season.

If he had a professional legacy, it was one of courtesy and a sense of humor, of a fine intelligence, but perhaps above all of enormously long hours and hard work.

A professional legacy is how your colleagues and peers will remember you after you've gone. What do you want your legacy to be?

The time to think about your professional legacy is not when they're planning your farewell party. You need to think about it much sooner—not from the beginning of your career, which is probably unlikely unless you're a savant with unusual skills and have always known what you want to do.

If you're like most people, you'll stumble along gradually getting better at some things, realizing that you'll never be great at others, and that there are a few things that you are really good at and hopefully also enjoy. That dawning usually coincides with a greater understanding of yourself, the good and the bad.

Thinking about your legacy can be useful at any time because it focuses your mind on what really matters to you.

Exercise 1: *Jot down what you'd like to be remembered for by your colleagues. Try to imagine you're writing the talking points for the host of your farewell reception. What are the qualities and achievements you'd like them to be describing when they talk about you?*

Think about your heroes. That's what Marshall Goldsmith did in an exercise run by Ayse Birsel.[5] Then he was challenged to be more like them.

Exercise 2: *Write a list of your heroes, personal and professional.*

Now write down their attributes. What were their chief characteristics?

Now cross out the names of your heroes and replace it with your own.

Here's what Marshall Goldsmith discovered: Each of his heroes had been extremely generous and a great teacher. To be more like his heroes, that's what he needed to be. That's why he began his 100 coaches project, in which he teaches 100 coaches everything he knows, for free, and ask them to pass it on.

Having done Exercises 1 and 2, you now have the road map for your professional legacy. Time to take action to secure it.

Leader Profile: Marshall Goldsmith

Marshall Goldsmith distinguishes success by internal and external factors.

Success factors

On the internal factors he says: "I love what I do. It increases my level of happiness. And I enjoy the process. I find it meaningful. That's my definition of success, doing what makes me happy and is meaningful.

"I really believe success is made up of five factors:

1. Health, you can't be successful if you're dead.
2. Wealth, you need a middle class lifestyle, but above that it doesn't make much difference.
3. Great relationships with people.
4. Happiness.
5. Meaning.

"I believe you have to have both happiness and meaning. Meaning without happiness is being a martyr, and happiness without meaning means you're just an empty shell. I'm very fortunate. I have all of those five things.

"On external factors, I have been lucky and worked with great people, like Dr. Paul Hersey who was once double booked and asked me to fill in for him at his client, Met Life. I did and did a great job. Luck alone isn't enough. Luck opens the door, then you have to deliver."

Six questions

"I have questions that I have a woman call me and ask me every day: whether I did my best, as a husband, as a father, whether I did my best to find meaning and be happy and so on."

Marshall's six questions are on his website at www.marshallgoldsmith.com.

Best advice

The best advice he didn't take? That would be from Paul Hersey again.

"I was doing really well and Paul said, "You're making too much money. You need to spend more time thinking and writing and then you can move to the next level and have a bigger impact."

"I didn't take that advice for 12 years. I did well but I repeated the same year over and over, like a hamster on wheel. If I had to do my life over, I would have listened to Paul and taken his advice sooner.

Be more like your heroes

"I was inspired to think about my legacy by Ayse Birsel, who asked me who my heroes were. I listed them: Frances Hesselbein, Richard Beckhard, Peter Drucker, Warren Bennis, and Alan Mulally, among others. They were all great teachers and they were all generous. She challenged me to be more like them. That's why I started the 15 coaches project, where I teach 15 people everything I know, for free, and they pass it on. That's now expanded to 100 coaches. I want to do for others what those great people did for me, for free, and then encourage them to do the same thing. It can only do more good than harm."

A Portfolio Career

I am often asked to help clients who want to build portfolio careers. Sometimes a firm will ask me to help a senior executive who will be retiring. Sometimes it is an individual who wants to position themselves for the next phase.

What exactly is a portfolio career, and how do you create one?

Let's assume you have had a great career and are currently in what will probably be your last full-time role. You are a little tired of corporate life and not really ready to retire but you don't want or need another full-time role. You know people who are serving on boards and acting as advisors to big-name firms. That looks attractive.

How do they do that?

The secret to building a successful portfolio career is being purposeful about creating it and clear about what really interests you. The old maxim of finding what you're good at and what you love applies here.

About 12 months before you are due to retire, go through your contacts and create a list of people who know you and could recommend you. Start calling them. Be transparent with them about what you're doing. That will make it easier for them to help you.

Develop a script: "We haven't spoken for a while. I wanted to let you know that I'm going to be stepping down from X, and I'm interested in board and advisory roles. I thought you would be a good person to advise me on that. Do you know of any? Would you be willing to recommend me?"

Then follow up. Set up meetings, coffees, and lunches. Talk to people. Talk to more people. Keep an open mind, but also keep your eye on the type of role you would ideally like. Don't commit to anything too fast, unless it's a dream role. Explore.

The best people to recommend you for board seats are peers or people senior to you in your industry. The second best are headhunters. Call the ones you know. If you don't know any, make a list of the big ones. Call them and ask to speak to the head of your industry's practice. Try to meet in person if you can.

Build your profile in your last year. Go to conferences, preferably as a speaker. Write about current topics in your industry for trade outlets. Update your LinkedIn profile. Get a decent headshot. Update your resume and get it laid out professionally.

Get a coach. This process is much easier if done with an experienced professional rather than on your own. My own clients speak highly of their experience:

> *"Corrie was an invaluable partner in my transition from public to private sector and move into the next phase of my professional life. With her supportive, direct manner she helped me discern between what I wanted to do and what others wanted to me to do, and to negotiate the various contracts and arrangements that constitute my professional life today. I highly recommend her."* —Evelyn N. Farkas, PhD, Former Deputy Assistant Secretary of Defense, United States

Important! Do not spend 100 percent of your time doing your current job. It doesn't matter how important it is or how busy things are. You should have built capacity for others to pick up your load. You need to be spending at least 20 percent of your time on building your new career. They will survive without you. Take care of your people, but make sure you don't do that at the expense of taking care of your future.

Follow this guidance and you will find you can easily turn your portfolio career into a portfolio life and enjoy its benefits and freedoms.

10

Sharing Is Caring, and Smart

I n a nutshell: It's not just nice to help others along the way, it's also smart. The benefits of a strong network are manifold, and good deeds are often returned in unexpected ways. Contributing to your network and those around you often rewards you more than them. But it's important to distinguish from an over-eagerness to help and problem-solve.

The Power of a Network

Scientists Lisa Berkman and Leonard Syme undertook the Alameda County study in 1979.[1] It was a nine-year study of the relation between social ties and mortality in one California county that would become one of the most important and impactful studies of its type.

What Berkman and Syme discovered was this: The fewer social ties people reported, the more likely they were to die over the nine-year period.

The difference between the mortality rates of those with the highest ties and those with the lowest was a whopping 2.3 times for men and 2.8 times for women.

In other words, the women with the fewest social ties were almost three times more likely to die over the period than the women with the most social ties.

The index of social ties included marriage, contacts with friends and relatives, organizational membership, and church membership.

Most intriguingly, the association between social ties and mortality was found to be independent of physical health, year of death, socioeconomic status, and health practices like smoking, alcohol consumption, obesity, or physical activity. In other words, weak social ties were a greater predictor of mortality than being overweight, drinking, or smoking!

The Alameda research spawned a multitude of studies that continue to explore and confirm the connection between social ties and health.

John Robbins, heir to the Baskin-Robbins ice cream fortune, walked away from the ice cream business to become a leader on environmental and health issues. He is the author of *No Happy Cows*, *The Good Life*, and *Diet for a New America.*

His book *Healthy at 100* surveys some of the longest-living communities around the world.[2] These included groups in Japan, Central Asia, Latin America, and the Caucasus. What he found those communities had in common was a diet that included plenty of whole grains, fruit and vegetables, and little processed foods, as well as a regime of daily vigorous exercise. No surprises there.

But what was less anticipated was that diet and exercise alone were not predictors of long life. Rather, Robbins found that the quality of personal relationships and social ties was extremely strong in the communities surveyed.

In all the communities studied, children and old people spent time together, often living in multigenerational units, friendships were highly valued, and the communal life of the society was extremely important. Isolated living was the exception.

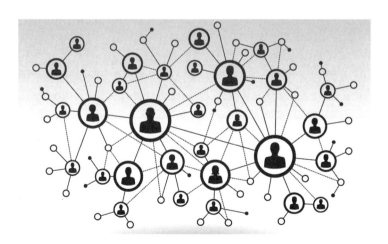

But those societies are not typical of the ones we live in. In Britain and the United States, roughly one in three people older than 65 live alone, and in the United States, half of those older than 85 live alone.

Loneliness is dramatically rising in Western society with devastating results, particularly among older people. In the UK, the Silver Line Helpline is a 24-hour call center for older adults seeking to fill a basic need: contact with other people.[3] It receives 10,000 calls a week, many from people who have not spoken to another person for days, or since the last time they called the center.

The poet Emily Dickinson described loneliness as "the horror not to be surveyed."[4] But it is an affliction that has gotten the attention of policymakers and government as the cost of loneliness because of the increasing evidence linking loneliness to physical illness and physical and mental decline. Some see that as the makings of an epidemic with serious consequences.

"The profound effects of loneliness on health and independence are a critical public health problem," said Dr. Carla M. Perissinotto, a geriatrician at the University of California, San Francisco.[5]

The implications from all this research should be clear: On the one end of the spectrum, we see the benefits of social networks and personal relationships, and at the other end, the pernicious harm of isolation.

Making an effort to build relationships, personal and professional, and be part of a community is not just good for your career—it can also save your life.

Leader Profile: Dr. Evelyn Farkas

Dr. Evelyn Farkas is the former Deputy Assistant Secretary of Defense for Russia, Ukraine, and Eurasia; a senior fellow at The Atlantic Council; a global business strategy consultant; and a national security analyst for NBC News. She appears frequently on MSNBC's top-rated television show "Morning Joe" to discuss national security issues. She attributes much of her success in life to the fact that her parents had fled the former Soviet bloc for life in the United States.

"I was the eldest child of Hungarian immigrants. I was a translator between two cultures. We were relatively less well off than most people in my town. For example, I didn't see *Star Wars* in the theater when it came out because my parents felt they couldn't afford to have us go. It wasn't a priority.... I think there was a drive to be at least on equal terms with the people I grew up with. That motivated me, and I had a sense of history, a sense that I had come from somewhere and I owed it to the people who had preceded me to be the best person I could be," she recalls.

"My grandparents had been writers and journalists in the Austro-Hungarian Empire. My relatives had served at court, one had been the treasurer of the empire, and another had saved the life of the emperor. They had served society and distinguished themselves. I grew up with a sense of belonging to a line of people who had done something meaningful with their lives and therefore I was also going to do something meaningful with my life," she explains.

Evelyn is an expert in foreign and defense policy. Among other things, she has served on the Senate Armed Services Committee staff, was executive director of a commission on WMD terrorism, and sat on the faculty of the U.S. Marine Corps Command and Staff College. She has monitored elections in Bosnia and Afghanistan. She has published a book, *Fractured States and U.S. Foreign Policy*, numerous articles, and speaks several languages. She has had to juggle competing priorities and digest large amounts of information in short amounts of time for much of her career.

"I make lists. First of all, I think ahead. What is it that I want to achieve? Then I break that down. I used to sometimes get overwhelmed, but I have a better handle on prioritization now. Making lists, not hesitating to ask people for advice or assistance. I've always been good at delegating as the oldest child. That's also important," she laughs.

What she wishes she had known earlier?

"I wish I had known that it's not just about hard work and building your resume, which I did and that is critical, but it's also about finding that person to work for who trusts you and likes you enough to pull you up with them. It's what they call sponsorship today," she says.

"When I was growing up we talked about mentors and those are people you went to for advice and that's all fine and good but those mentors, they might pass you along from person to person but they're not necessarily going to give you your next job. I realized that it is actually far more valuable to find someone who will give you your next job," she explains.

On what to do when you're in a role, Evelyn's view has evolved.

"I used to downplay how much the interpersonal mattered, meaning how well you get along with people or with your bosses. But I've seen now, as an older professional, how important it is to senior people that they like the people they're working with. And they get to choose who they work with," she notes.

"To be likeable is not always easy because at work you're usually focusing, and you have to be excellent, which means sometimes you're not likeable or sometimes there's a tension between being likeable and being excellent at your job. But it's really important to get along well with people," she added.

On the hallmarks of her brand, especially as she expands into media and public commentary:

"I'm known for being able to make complicated issues comprehensible to people and for articulating myself clearly and directly. I think, if anything, people know me as a straight shooter. I'm fair, but I'm a straight shooter," she observes.

In terms of downtime, Evelyn pauses to reflect.

"I have no hobbies!" she laughs. "What do I do to renew myself? I run, I read fiction. I go out with friends, because I'm a real extrovert. I run, generally, every other day about four or five miles. And I also do weight lifting, but that's not so much for rejuvenation. I take long walks to clear my head.

Advice for others?

"Don't be afraid to put some money on the line to hire competent help," she says. "When I left government, I invested in an executive coach, you, Corrie, and I invested in my lawyer, Deneen Howell. She's really impressive and I said to myself: 'Okay. You're a big girl now, hire the big lawyer. Do it right,'" she laughs.

Leverage Your Competitive Streak

"I'm a connector. I always have been. I love to introduce people to each other. I love to connect ideas as well; call it lateral thinking. It makes me happy. It felt strange putting it on my resume as a skill, but it is a skill. I'm good at this and I enjoy it," said Sabine Hertveldt, a Belgian lawyer who works for the World Bank in Washington.

Sabine is known for introducing people across her professional and social network. She's good at building and maintaining relationships, and she's generous with her time. You go to Sabine to bounce an idea around and leave with introductions to three people who can help move the idea along.

We don't always think of this as a valuable skill, but it is. Making connections and bringing people together is, in fact, a lucrative business for many lobbyists and consultants.

But often people who are good at this don't think of it as expertise in the same way as their professional skills and qualifications.

If building relationships is a skill of yours, then you need to leverage it. Relationship building and networking is important for your career as well as your well-being, as we've just explored. Use that skill to gain a competitive advantage at work and to build your social capital across your life.

Your relationships are a form of social capital. You invest and build that capital over time. It's predicated on trust, reciprocity, and cooperation.

Here are some ways to build social capital and strengthen your relationships:

1. **Listen well.** Everyone benefits from the balm of a good listen. Next time you're with a friend or someone with whom you're trying to build a relationship, listen more and talk less. If you

find that hard, try repeating the last phrase the person says to you. For example, when a colleague is talking about how difficult the project they're working on is and finishes up by saying: "I don't know how I am going to get it done by the deadline," you simply reply "You don't know if you'll be able to get it done by the deadline?" This sounds redundant, but you'll see they will continue with the thought and probably add more information. They will also feel well understood and listened to. It's also easy on you and a simple habit to get into.

2. **Assume good intent.** When the person with whom you're trying to build or strengthen a relationship does something irritating or annoying, give them the benefit of the doubt. Assume they did not set out to purposely annoy you. Then explore why they did what they did to understand their perspective. It's rare to find a person who gets up in the morning with the intent of messing things up for others or hurting them. We assume our actions are always justified and reasonable, so why not extend that assumption to others?

3. **Stay in touch.** This is easier and easier with social networks, email, and other forms. Drop a line to let the person know you were thinking of them. You can do this with people who

used to be in senior roles in your professional life but have now moved on. You might not have thought of dropping your CEO a line when you saw an interesting article, but now they've left the company; why not? You know them and it's an easy way to stay connected. The same goes for an annual holiday card or seasonal note. It doesn't have to be a lengthy brag fest of all your accomplishments, but a short mailing with a photo keeps you top of mind of people you don't see as often as you'd like. You can easily generate envelope labels from your contacts to make it less of a chore.

4. **Standing by in hard times.** The true test of friendship and depth of a relationship is standing by in hard times. It's easy to be a good friend when things are going well, but when your friend is having a hard time and acting out by being cranky and difficult, that's when your character shows up. Do you stick with them when they need you or are you hard to find in their darkest days? A former colleague had lost his job in ignominious circumstances. An unpleasant boss had forced him out, but the boss was still around and we all still worked for him. The colleague says he remembered clearly who had been supportive and checked in on him during that difficult time, especially

as his career rebounded and many former colleagues would later petition him for roles in his new organization.

5. **Short and sweet.** The easiest way to keep your relationships fresh and build that social capital is to be in touch frequently but briefly. If you keep putting off that catch-up call, you'll feel obliged to chat for 30 minutes or to visit in person when you don't have the time. Instead, send a quick email or text message to let them know you're thinking of them and hope they're doing well. If you simply say they were on your mind, you don't even leave them with a question they feel obliged to answer. You've sent a little gift. Connection made. Relationship maintained. Onward.

Better to Give Than Receive

I used to mentor a lawyer at my old firm as part of an official mentoring program. I was head of communications and didn't deal too often with the legal staff, except when clients got into trouble and it threatened to spill into the public domain. I thought I was doing this guy a favor. He was new to the organization and in a part of it with a fairly narrow relationship to the business.

How wrong was I! Every time we met, I would leave with new intelligence and insights into parts of the business to which I would normally not be privy. I heard about personalities and processes that I was unaware of and learned a lot about how that part of the business functioned.

He enjoyed our conversations as well and found my broader perspective and institutional knowledge gathered over many years to be useful and interesting, but I was always left with the feeling that the net gain was mine.

The phrase "Better to give than receive" is a reformulation of the Bible verse "It is more blessed to give than receive," found in the New Testament in Acts 20:35.[6]

It is a phrase that has come into common use because it holds true across such widespread activities. People who mentor others, whether professionally or privately, regularly talk about the pleasure it gives them and how they benefit in unexpected ways.

I know a woman who signed up to mentor a teen mother who was determined to enter and complete college. The teenager, Carmen, was the first person in her family to graduate high school, never mind college. Carmen found the process somewhat daunting and enjoyed having a mentor who understood what office hours were and the pressure of studying for exams. At times, the mentor felt overwhelmed at the obstacles her mentee faced and worried that she might get drawn into solving every problem. That was not the case. The mentee was extremely motivated and organized. She kept herself on track with support from family, but they both came to enjoy their monthly lunches at a local Chinese restaurant.

"I never fail to leave feeling inspired by Carmen and realizing that I have had it so easy in life. I walk away thinking *I* can do anything and that there's no limit to what *I* can do in my life if I set my mind to it," the mentor told me.

The irony in the situation did not escape her. She was supposed to be inspiring and supporting Carmen, not the other way around.

It's not just giving our time to others that benefits us; the same is true of giving our money. A report on how spending on others pays off determined that people experienced higher rates of happiness when they spent money on others rather than on themselves.[7] The scientific term is "prosocial spending." And it seems that people all over the world, even toddlers, can experience a warm glow from spending on others.

The scientists think the reason for that has to do with the fact that spending on others meets some core human needs like relatedness, competence, and autonomy. They saw the rewards show up in both the body and the brain.

See if it works for you. Next time you buy something for yourself, whether it's a coffee, bunch of flowers, or a bottle of wine, pick up an extra one and give it to someone. Spontaneously. Now see how you feel.

I know I get immense pleasure when I pick up a "Giving Tree" star at our local church at Christmas. It's a project to make sure low-income children in our town get presents at Christmas. You get the first name, age, and gender of the child and their wish list. It includes clothes and shoe sizes, so you can buy something practical as well. I find myself really enjoying shopping for the children and worrying about whether the gifts will be what they had in mind and if they will get more or less than their class-mates. It's not a solution to the poverty in our city, but I know if it benefits them to receive the gifts half as much as it benefits me to give, then more good than harm has been done.

These results also have a lasting benefit. Just recall-ing the time you did something nice for someone or said something that made someone happy recreates the warm glow in the giver. Try it. You'll be surprised how good it leaves you feeling.

Amos Tversky, the renowned Israeli psychologist, was described by Michael Lewis in his 2016 book *The Undoing Project* as having a theory of socializing: Because stingi-ness and generosity are both contagious, and because behaving generously makes you happier, surround your-self with generous people.[8]

Give generously. It will do you good.

When Not to Help

Do you suffer from predilection to help? Do you offer advice to people who didn't ask for it? Do you problem-solve and offer to fix things for others as a default setting? Do you find yourself getting involved in people's lives and being pulled in as their complications increase?

You may be suffering from "predilection to help." It's a common phenomenon. You're a caring sort. You're quite good at getting things done. You have a strong sense of fairness or justice. You like to help others. It makes you feel useful and it's an important value to you. It's part of who you are.

But a predilection to help can be as much a strength as a weakness.

A good friend is the designated caregiver among her siblings. She's the one who rallies the others to travel for family gatherings. She often hosts everyone at her house. She calls regularly to check in on parents in Boston, and siblings in New York and on the West Coast. She's good at remembering birthdays and graduations. As her parents have aged, the role she has given herself has gotten larger and larger.

They are now in and out of the hospital and doctors' offices. They need help navigating the health care system, managing prescriptions and appointments, hiring and firing paid caregivers, and soon, moving into assisted living.

None of the siblings live in the same town as the parents, so, in theory, the playing field for helping them is level. But it's become a default that my friend does the heavy lifting. She then becomes resentful, as her own life is already full with work and family.

These are tasks that must be attended to, in her opinion, and if they don't get done her parents will suffer, and she doesn't want that, as she loves them very much.

This may not be an issue for you, and if it's not, skip ahead. But if you recognize yourself as someone prone to bear more than their fair share of a given situation, take a step back and see if the problem is with you.

"I used to think she just had a lot on her plate but now I realize that there's always drama about something. Someone always needs her urgently. Things go wrong, people don't show up, and then she has to fill the gap. I have given up relying on her. If I make a plan to meet her, I always have a back-up in mind in case she cancels. I'm very reluctant to recommend her for work because she does the same thing to clients."

That's what a British ad executive told me one day about a mutual colleague. It had taken us both years to realize that there was a pattern and that our friend, for whatever reason, would always get sucked into family dramas and the need to help others while her friendships, quality of life, and career took the hit.

This is why it matters. If you enjoy rescuing people and being the one to solve every problem and can still maintain relationships with the people you love and keep your business or career on track, then great. There's no problem.

But if, like our friend, you are actually losing work and jeopardizing your social ties because you get so overinvolved in helping others, then maybe it's time to take a closer look.

See how many of these statements apply to you:

1. I am always the one to leave work when there's a problem at home.
2. I do more than my siblings in caring for others in our family.
3. I never refuse a friend who asks me for help.
4. I regularly have to rearrange my schedule for an unexpected personal event.
5. I always make the last response when debating issues by email.
6. People sometimes forget that I said I would do something for them when I do it.

If more than three of these apply to you, you may be suffering from "predilection to help." It's pretty common and often relates to underlying issues about control. It's easy to identify, but hard to treat.

Here are three tips to try to curb your predilection to help:

1. Wait 24 hours before replying to a request for help.
2. Ask the person with the issue what they think they should do.
3. Say you can't help and see what happens.

Hint: Do not do any of these with your boss. This is for personal and so-called emergency requests.

Keep practicing. Getting over this affliction will free you up and give you more opportunity to focus on the things that are really important and the things you want to achieve in your life.

The Pursuit of Learning

"If you're not learning, you're not growing," a former mentor told me. He was completely committed to lifelong learning, to self-reinvention, and had a boundless curiosity about the world and people.

It matters more than we think. We've all read the articles that tell us it's important to keep our brains active, but how often do we feel inclined to do that at the end of a long day when Netflix and the couch beckon?

The data on this is pretty robust, and the results are interesting. It turns out we need to be challenged in order to remain mentally nimble as we age.

If you look around, you'll see great variations in the mental capacity of older people. Some experience the usual onset of forgetfulness and loss of attention span, while others remain sharp and fully engaged in challenging pursuits.

These people have the mental capacity of people much younger than themselves and are called superagers. They are the subject of research undertaken by Lisa Feldman Barrett at Northeastern University.[9] The research showed that in superagers the "hub" areas of the brain like the limbic system, which are responsible for many functions including emotion, language, and stress, were much thicker than in other people of similar age.

The reason for that thickness was that their brains were working harder.

Feldman Barrett and her colleagues found that superagers were regularly challenged, physically and mentally. They engaged in vigorous exercise and strenuous mental effort. And they made an effort well past the point of pleasant.

The difficulty, of course, is that making that level of effort is hard and we want to stop. But the research shows that is exactly when the benefits kick in. We have to press on and make more of an effort than we want to in order to reap the benefits.

Our culture conspires to have us avoid pain and seek happiness. We are not fans of delayed gratification. But experiencing pain in this instance is in fact helpful to our lifelong health. Our brain tissue gets thinner from disuse.

Learning something new and challenging yourself physically and mentally is the key to better aging and a more fulfilling life. Exercising the brain ensures you keep it in good shape and, like with the rest of our body, it's never too early to start.

There are innumerable activities you could take up in order to challenge yourself. Skip the easy pleasure of Sudoku and find something that actually challenges your brain. Take up a new sport. Learn a foreign language. Sign up for a college course. Master a musical instrument.

Factor in practice; consider getting an instructor or joining a club to make it easier for you to continue to make the effort needed. Work that brain!

11

Imagine the Unimaginable

I *n a nutshell: Why not do something that pays more, is more* *interesting, and takes less time than your current job? That* *seems impossible, but maybe it's not. The same goes for that* *really big role. Why not you? How hard could it be? The* *person doing it now is also a mortal. Setting your sights on* *the unimaginable will give you impetus for change and get-* *ting there.*

The Biggest Job

When you talk to people who have really big jobs, they will often say that before they took on the role they weren't sure they could do it.

"When you're looking further up the ladder, you always think, 'What is it that they've got that I haven't?'

Well, there's not anything. Probably just experience and confidence," said Jenny Scott, executive director at The Bank of England.

If you have the experience, why not apply for that senior role? You can quickly find out if others think you're qualified. You won't get it, if they don't. If you have doubts about your own ability, why not trust theirs? Trust them to make a good decision.

A former colleague was approached by her boss to take on a more senior role. She baulked. She couldn't imagine taking on any more responsibility. She had young children and worked a four-day week, which she liked. The current job was demanding and interesting. She really wasn't looking to make any changes.

Her boss persisted. He said the role could be adapted and done in four days. He thought she was the best person for the role and wanted her to take a chance. She still hesitated.

She was flattered, but when she looked at who her new peers would be, she felt daunted. These were people she had looked up to, people to whom she had always been more junior, and now she would be a peer?

But her boss would not be dissuaded, and, after giving her plenty of time to think about it and several more encouraging conversations, he finally persuaded her and she decided to give it a go.

It went well. So well, in fact, that a couple of years later she was tapped again and asked to be chief of staff for a new CEO. She maintained the four-day work week throughout.

A good friend gave me some very useful advice many years ago. She said that the job that appears daunting and too hard will never be as hard again as it is in the beginning. The first week or month will be the hardest, and it will gradually get easier. The second week will be a little less difficult, the second month less hard than the first, and so on.

It's almost like a law of physics that it can't remain new indefinitely. And by becoming more familiar, it becomes easier, by definition.

The other thing that becomes apparent when you take a big job is that those colleagues you used to admire from afar are only human. That's what my former colleague discovered when she became a peer of colleagues who had long been her senior. She even discovered that some of them were not as talented as she had assumed. Weaknesses and foibles became clearer with closer quarters and she realized that she was in fact every inch their peer.

Once you take a significantly senior role in an organization, it can often be quite eye opening at how poorly run things are, jarring with the perception you held as an outsider. If you always assumed there were smarter people somewhere making better decisions, it can be a shock to discover that's not the case and in fact you have a lot to contribute to making things go better.

Perhaps that's why they hired you?

Leader Profile: Jenny Scott

Jenny Scott is an executive director at the Bank of England, where she is responsible for all the Bank's external communications and is an advisor to Governor Mark Carney. Her time at the Bank has coincided with some of the most tumultuous years in global finance, including the global financial crisis, subsequent Eurozone crisis, and most recently Brexit.

Jenny began her career at the Bank of England, then left to pursue a career in journalism with Reuters and BBC television as their economic correspondent before returning to the Bank in 2008.

"For me, the biggest game-changer in my career, the thing that made the difference, was confidence. And that's the thing that I wish I'd known earlier, that I can actually do it. I knew that on a sort of intellectual basis, but I thought that there was a secret ingredient that I just didn't know or that there must be more to it than this," she recalls.

"Under-promise, over-deliver has always been my mantra although there's a version of under-promise and over-deliver that is born out of insecurity and lack of confidence; and there's an alternative, which is a more mature approach to that, which I think of as servant leadership, which is still having humility, but not false humility or false modesty," she explains.

"I know it when I see it in others and I think it's incredibly powerful. It's about empowering others from a position of strength," she says.

"I've realized as I've got older that, for me, it's important to be more deliberate in things. And I mean that in relation to life as a whole, not just a career. Life is busy and there are certain times, seasons in your life, when you're incredibly busy and you can just sort of get swept along by things. I think there's an awful lot to be gained in stopping, assessing, thinking and being deliberate," she explains.

Although she admits she didn't always have a big picture of what she wanted to do.

"I never used to have a plan. I knew I really liked economics, but that was as far as my thinking went. I never thought, 'I want to be an economics reporter or correspondent.' And I certainly never thought, 'I'm going to be successful.'" Good Lord, no," she says laughing. "I still don't think of myself like that at all. Partly because I'm surrounded by people who, in many respects, are way more successful than I am," she adds.

Her definition of success?

"Success is obviously not your pay packet or how many people report to you, and it's not how big your corner office is. That's such an outdated, superficial definition for me. It's much more about getting all of the balances right. Challenging yourself but not to the point where you're stressed out. Being busy but not to the point where you've got no energy left. Having a fulfilling job but not to the point where you have no private personal life. If you've got kids, having happy kids alongside. It's not having the balance skewed in any way. It's doing everything you can to the best of your ability, but also nurturing yourself in the meantime," she says.

Jenny is married to Mike and has twin six-year-old girls, whom the couple adopted from Russia in 2011.

"For me, happiness is like success and it's like money. It's a byproduct of doing the right thing and being in tune with your life. And just like everyone else, I certainly don't always get that right by any means."

In terms of how she manages such a large portfolio at work, Jenny says it's down to two key things:

"I have a fantastic assistant, Sarah. We're in tune with each other. I trust her implicitly. She anticipates what I need. We've been working together a long time, now. The quid pro quo is that I try to give her interesting work and as much responsibility as she wants. Then the second thing is having deputies who are better than you are! My two heads of division are outstanding. We have a shared vision. We are all agreed on what we're trying to achieve and the principles we're trying to achieve them by," she explains.

"Another thing that's important for me is that I work part-time, four days a week. The reality is that I stay across my work on that day off, but it gives me some modicum of control over my life and the ability to do other things on that day, which all adds to the balance," she notes.

And in terms of rejuvenation, she enjoys spending time with her family and fitting in exercise.

"Exercise is important to me. I cycle to work and sometimes at the weekends. If I don't have some exercise I would go a bit mad. And I've recently started taking tennis lessons," she told me.

"I saw a documentary recently about aging and the narrator was 75 years old and still playing tennis and I thought, "That's what I need to do." It's a sociable sport. I'm learning a new skill, getting a bit of exercise. It's great fun. I'm really enjoying that," she adds, smiling broadly.

Check Out the Competition

One way to determine whether you're ready for a major step up in career is to check out the competition. Survey the market and see if you're on par with people who are in the positions you aspire to hold.

The easiest way to check the market is to apply to more-senior positions and see what happens.

Dust off your resume, have a reliable friend take a look at it and then look for open positions. Look further afield than your city or country. Check out listings in publications like *The Economist* and online vacancy sections of large organizations and companies. If you're intention is to scope the market, rather than actually make a move now, going further afield is a good move. It's less likely that people will know you and that your current employer finds out you're looking elsewhere. This is not the time to post on LinkedIn, for example.

If you are called to interview, do your best, see if they move you forward to the next round and then pull out if you're not interested in actually taking the role.

Caveat: Do not lead employers on. If you have no intention of taking the role, don't go past a preliminary discussion or two. While it is flattering to be shortlisted and offered a job, it is extremely disrespectful to waste an employer's time and energy if you have no intention of taking the job. It's also damaging to your reputation.

Many positions are found via recruiters, also known as headhunters. You should have a relationship with a couple of recruiters and be in irregular contact with them. They tend to stay in their industry but move from firm to firm, so staying in touch is important.

Recruiters work on a transactional basis and have little or no interest in you unless you fit the profile of a role they are currently filling. That's why you need to apply to vacant roles. You want to meet them or speak with them and build a relationship so that you're in their Rolodex (can we still say that?) for the future. When a new role comes up, they comb through that Rolodex for prospective candidates and that's where they find you!

Applying to vacant positions to see if you get called to interview achieves a number of things:

1. You refresh your resume and take stock of your experience.
2. You get outside of your bubble to see opportunities beyond your own company.
3. You get a sense of your value in the market at a point in time.
4. You can compare your remuneration against the market and see if you're being fairly paid.

Other ways to check out if you're ready for a much larger role is to talk to people in those roles. Ask senior people in your organization, and among your friends and neighbors, for 30 minutes of their time to talk about what they do and how they got there.

Most people will be flattered if you say you admire them and are trying to better understand what it takes to be in a senior role. Invite them for coffee and listen carefully.

Here are some questions you can ask:

1. Why do you think you've been so successful in your career?
2. What are some of the people, incidents or decisions that led to this point?
3. What are your secrets to getting a lot done?
4. What do you wish you had known earlier in life?

If you've been in your company for a long time, you need to examine if that's working against your professional progress. There is a phenomenon I've noticed of people who effectively "grow up" in an organization, meaning they join at a junior or mid-level and spend some of their most formative professional years at the same institution.

Even if they progress well, it's unlikely to be at the same pace as if they had moved around among different companies. That's not necessarily a negative; if you enjoy your work, your colleagues and the work is interesting and rewarding, there are plenty of reasons to stay somewhere despite a lack of rapid promotion.

Where it's a problem is when your colleagues or members of the senior team still see you as that junior person who first joined and don't view you as they would if you showed up as a new hire today.

This happens particularly frequently to women. Their colleagues still regard them as the person who joined 10 years ago, despite the considerable experience and skill they've accumulated in the intervening years. Very often, women themselves don't realize their increased value because they are seeing an inaccurate reflection in how their colleagues view them.

That's why a reality check and testing the waters externally can be so valuable. You don't know your own worth until you check the market!

Find Role Models

We've talked about having sponsors and mentors, and the difference between them. Sponsors can actually give you new roles and take you with them to other companies. Mentors encourage and advise you.

Role models provide another form of inspiration and ideas.

The definition of a role model, according to Webster's dictionary is, "A person who serves as an example of the values, attitudes, and behaviors associated with a role. For example, a father is a role model for his sons. Role models can also be persons who distinguish themselves in such a way that others admire and want to emulate them."[1]

When you talk with successful people, they will often talk about their own role models. Oftentimes, this is a parent or their first boss. Very often, the role model wasn't as conventionally successful as the person they provided inspiration to.

Adam Bryant has a weekly column in the *New York Times* called "Corner Office." In it, he profiles leaders across the United States in both corporate and nonprofit areas. One recurring theme is the important impact a parent had as a role model for many of the leaders profiled. The column is a worthwhile read for professional inspiration and to see the variety of role models for different leaders.

I worked with Dr. Nafis Sadik, a Pakistani doctor and head of the United Nations agency for reproductive health, UNFPA, in the mid-1990s. She was an extraordinarily courageous and successful leader of that agency and, at 87 years of age, still works for the United Nations as a Special Advisor to the UN Secretary General.

Nafis credited her father with being an important influence on her career because of his support and encouragement that she get a good education. For a middle-class girl growing up in India and subsequently Pakistan, that was not the norm. Marriage and family were considered the extent of a girl's ambitions. She would go on to become a medical doctor and ultimately lead a UN agency that reshaped the global discussion about the rights of women and adolescents to control their fertility and plan their families.

You may not be as fortunate to have someone encouraging you from an early age to fulfill your potential. I am reminded of a man in his late 50s whom I met recently who told me he was not good at having role models or mentors because he had lost his father early in life and therefore wasn't used to being given advice. He admired other colleagues who did seek out others for advice. I guess he had never considered the possibility that their fathers may have given poor advice or none at all, but they persisted in finding mentors nonetheless.

Regardless of whether you grew up with someone you admired and who encouraged you, there are plenty of ways you can acquire role models to whom you can look up to. Here are some suggestions:

1. **Read biographies of famous people.** Notice their characteristics. Look for behaviors that contributed to their success. If you enjoy history, go back in time and read the lives of eminent people. If you want something that resonates more with modern life, you're spoiled for choice in recent biographies of leaders in business and public life.

2. **Look for role models in your workplace.** Who seems to have things sorted? Who is successful professionally and also seems to be a decent human being with a life?

3. **Look among your neighbors and friends.** Your role model doesn't need to be a titan of industry or former head of state. Learn more about what your friends and neighbors have done professionally. You may be surprised by what you learn.

If you can spend time with potential role models, so much the better. Ask them about their philosophy or most important values. What do they hold dear? Inquire about the habits they think made them productive and successful.

Post a picture of your role model or role models above your desk. It's helpful have a visual prompt of the person who inspires you to seep into your subconscious.

I'm a great fan of Theodore Roosevelt and keep a picture of him and the text of "The Man in the Arena," an excerpt from his most famous speech, "Citizenship in a Republic," [2] on my fridge. His speech praises the person taking action and trying to achieve their goals—"the man in the arena"—rather than those who stand on the sidelines criticizing and second guessing, "those cold and

timid souls." I don't necessarily read it every time I reach for the milk, but I'm sure his image and words have a positive, encouraging impact.

Entrepreneurship

Those who follow the siren call of entrepreneurship are among the bravest of souls, in my opinion. I confess to being biased on this score as an entrepreneur myself.

Entrepreneurship is on the rise after several years of declining numbers following the global financial crisis of 2008.

Globally, around 12% of the working-age population, that's 320 million people, are engaged in early-stage entrepreneurship in the G20 countries.[3] Many of those are in China and India. Entrepreneurship in the United States is slowly regaining the ground lost because of the financial crisis, but the rate of new businesses being created had been slowing down well before the crisis.

According to the U.S. Census Bureau, the share of private firms less than a year old has dropped from more than 12% during much of the 1980s to only about 8% since 2010. And the trend is heading down. The most recent data is for 2014, which is the second lowest on record, after 2010.[4] And the share of employees working at start-up businesses is also dropping, from 4% to 2% of private sector jobs.[5]

That bad news does not dissuade those who want to strike out on their own. It also may not cover the growing "gig economy," which is made up of individuals working freelance or solo. If those individuals don't register as businesses, they may not be captured by the data.

The lure of entrepreneurship is strong, and while many think about setting up their own business only a tiny minority ever actually does so.

There are a couple of basic models for entrepreneurship. The classic involves setting up a business to meet an identified need and hiring people to help produce the product or service you're selling. Often the goal is to grow the business as large as possible, and then sell it or hand it down to family members.

The alternative is the solo entrepreneur, often also a consultant. This model relies on the skills of the individual who does not have employees, though he or she may outsource some tasks. In this model, there are no employees to keep on payroll and nothing to sell to someone else. When the person stops working, the business goes away.

At the higher end of the "gig economy," you'll find consultants who are more accurately described as entrepreneurs than as "freelancers" or "contractors."

Despite the gloomy statistics, there are plenty of people willing to make the leap. The greatest attraction is the freedom and autonomy as well as potential to make more money than you would as a salaried employee. While there is more risk, there is also the potential for more reward.

Embracing entrepreneurship means embracing risk, ambiguity and uncertainty. It requires resilience, commitment and plain stubbornness. The few who do make it have these traits. The rewards can be much more meaningful than money.

"The best way to predict the future is to create it."
—Peter Drucker

If you are considering entrepreneurship, you'll need the following five things:

1. **Talent**—You need to have something to offer and to be good at demonstrating its value to others.
2. **Market**—It's impossible to truly test a market without actually setting up. People will say anything in a focus group. Do as much due diligence as you can, and if there are others in your market talk to them.
3. **Passion**—Almost by definition, entrepreneurship is harder than just showing up to work every day. You have to make it count every day and be really committed to your own success.
4. **Support**—This includes financial and emotional support, but of these two emotional support is the most important. You need people in your corner to rally you when you're down and who believe in you completely.
5. **Urgency**—Probably the worst handicap for an entrepreneur is a big, soft safety net. If you

don't have the pressure of making payroll or your mortgage payments, you'll find it hard to create real momentum quickly.

Forward Motion

Isaac Newton's first law of physics is sometimes known as the law of inertia.

"An object at rest stays at rest and an object in motion stays in motion with the same speed and in the same direction unless acted upon by an unbalanced force."[6]

What this means is that objects tend to keep doing what they are doing. It means there is a natural tendency for objects to resist changes in their state of motion. That's why it's also known as the law of inertia. If an object is doing nothing, it will continue to do nothing, unless something comes along to change that.

This applies as well to us as to animate objects! Think about it. It's often easier to make change when you are forced to by circumstances, an external force. Think of the person who has a heart attack and decides to embrace a healthy diet and exercise, having never done so before. Or the person who loses their job, which they didn't enjoy, and is then forced to find something different.

That's the first part of the law, that it takes an external object to move us out of the inertia of our current situation. The second is just as intriguing.

An object in motion will stay in motion, unless impacted by another object. That's the law of momentum. If we are moving at speed, we can keep going until something stops us.

That has implications for us in terms of what we want to achieve in life. If we get ourselves moving and develop good habits, we should be able to keep going. We may get knocked off course now and then, but the point of Newton's law is that it is harder to stop us than to start us off in the first place.

Another good maxim in this regard is that it is better to move three things forward a mile than 10 things forward an inch.

We tend to be widely over-optimistic in estimating our own willpower. That's why New Year's resolutions and diets rarely work. The very number of things we aim to do better—eat less, save more, go to the gym and so on—reduces our ability to make any real change.

Pick three things you'd like to improve and give yourself a realistic time frame for getting them done, and start making them a habit. It takes an estimated 21 days for a new habit to stick.

Once you're up and running, you'll have momentum on your side and a far greater chance of keeping going.

Jot down now the three things you'd most like to change, and start putting the laws of physics in your favor. You'll be surprised by what you can achieve.

12

Reflect, Renew, Repeat

*I*n a nutshell: Once you have embarked on this path and are beginning to create the life and career you truly desire, you need regular milestones and sustenance as you go. Build it in now, before you start. Like an athlete on race day, you'll see the markers up ahead and know there will be water coming soon. Set aside time for reflection to see the progress you've made, adjust course as needed and enjoy. You are doing what you really want to be doing and life is rich and good.

Keep Up the Momentum

Let's assume you've started making changes in your life and are heading in the right direction. You've set some goals and are working toward achieving them. You've stopped trying to find "work–life balance," a ridiculous concept that suggests teetering at some midpoint from which you will surely get dislodged.

Instead, you're treating your life as one, as one great life and an integrated one, not two opposing lives in conflict with each other.

You have forward motion. You're trying to enjoy the present and the journey and ignore the voice in your head that says: "you'll be happy when..."

How do you keep this momentum?

We know from Isaac Newton that once started, momentum is hard to stop. How then do you retain it and recover from the obstacles that conspire to knock you off course?

Here are some of the tools in your arsenal:

1. **Meditation**: Become aware of the anxious thoughts that crowd in and threaten to undermine your resolve. The more awareness you can bring to what's happening in your mind, the greater stability of mind you can maintain. Stability of the mind is a great antidote to those anxious thoughts. Left to themselves, they will fester and grow. Like a drunken monkey in your brain, you need to step back and notice your thoughts. They are not you; they are just thoughts. They come and they can go.

2. **Prayer:** If you have a religious faith and don't already have a daily morning ritual of prayer,

try to set a daily practice. It will set the tenor of your day. The more regular and routine you make it, the more you'll notice when you're feeling off course or anxious. Let the power of your faith guide you through the more difficult periods of life.

3. **Transcendence**: Cultivate moments of transcendence, those moments when you look up above the quotidian and purposefully seek to lift your spirit. You can find transcendence in plenty of nonreligious venues. For example, joining others in communal song is both comforting and restorative. Transcendence is out there; you just need to look for opportunities to experience it.

4. **Nature**: Being in nature is a great way to find transcendence. Regardless of the weather, there is beauty in Mother Nature. Notice the sounds on an early morning walk. Look up to notice those things we tend not to see. Leave your phone behind.

5. **Exercise**: Those endorphins are not just good for your body, they are also beneficial to your spirit. Making exercise routine will help maintain a level of well-being that you can draw on when you get down.

6. **Journaling**: Keeping a journal can help you stay on track and keep up momentum. Note

what you are thankful for, what's going well and what you've accomplished. It's probably more than you think, even if it's not all that you want. A journal is a great place to note when you're feeling sad or downhearted. Looking back at those moments in a journal reminds you that those difficult feelings and situations pass.

Rewards and Grace

As a culture, we tend to be very hard on ourselves. We think that if only we tried harder things would come about the way we want. Hard work is necessary and we've explored the value of effort and habit earlier in this book. But there is also a time for reward and giving oneself a break.

There are a number of reasons to do this:

1. Continuous effort without rest and reward leads to diminishing returns over time. In effect you are wearing yourself down.
2. Rest and reflection result in some of our most productive and creative moments. That's why people talk about having great ideas in the shower.
3. It's really hard on the people around you. If you are continually hard on yourself, what signal are you sending to the people on your team and your family members?

I know a senior executive who takes a weekly "sabbatical" to think about his life and business. He schedules two hours on a Friday afternoon when he doesn't take any meetings or calls. He closes the door and sits back to reflect on how the week went, what he accomplished and what he didn't get done. He'll consider how he was that week, whether he had been present and aware, and if he had been a good boss, good friend, and so on.

If you can't do that during the work week, find a time on the weekend, maybe early on Saturday or Sunday morning before your day starts, to think about the week that was and what you'd like from the week ahead. Musing without an agenda can prompt surprising insights. Keep a piece of paper or journal handy to catch some of those more useful thoughts.

"If I spent as much time acting on the things I care about as I do worrying and thinking about them, I'd be in a much better place," a coaching client once told me. "I spent an inordinate amount of time with my wheels spinning internally, but have little or nothing to show for it."

You can use rewards as a system to keep yourself motivated and on track. They don't just work with pets and children. Rewards are a legitimate psychological tool to encourage yourself.

As you plan your week or day, think about ways to reward yourself for completing tasks or starting difficult projects. Jot down your rewards opposite the task. You can also put these on your calendar right after you finish the task.

Here's what it might look like:

Task	Reward
Strategy Memo	Coffee
Conversation with weak performer	Walk
Workout	Smoothie

Task	Reward
9 a.m. - Strategy Memo	10 a.m. - Coffee
10:30 a.m. - Conversation with weak performer	11:30 a.m. - Walk
4 p.m. - Workout	5 p.m. - Smoothie

Some of the tasks here might be rewards, and even vice versa, but figure out what you're procrastinating about, schedule some time to do it and then schedule the reward. You'll feel so much more motivated to get through the task to get to the reward. Scheduling prevents you from skipping straight to the reward and builds in the habit of effort and reward, which becomes a positive, motivating cycle.

Exercise: *Write a list of things you want to get done or need to start. Now write some of your favorite rewards and treats. Then pair them proportionally. Finishing that major report gets you a night out at a game or a massage. Clearing a closet or drafting a short memo is worth a nice cup of coffee with no distractions.*

Reflection

Motivation comes in two forms, extrinsic and intrinsic. Extrinsic motivation is when you do something for an external reward or to avoid negative consequences. For example, at a restaurant you pass on the steak in favor of fish because you know it's better for you. Intrinsic motivation is when you do something for its own sake, because you enjoy it or find it interesting. You order the fish because you like fish.

Psychologists will argue that intrinsic motivation is "better" because it is innate, doesn't rely on external factors and is well, intrinsic. That's true to a point, but the extrinsic becomes intrinsic with practice.

Think of our example: if you keep ordering the fish because it is better for you and you start to feel or look better as a result, your motivation to choose it may shift to being intrinsic. I want the fish because I like how I feel afterwards.

You can use reflection to clarify your motivations and see which ones might be moved from extrinsic to intrinsic over time.

Reflection is also a powerful tool in tracking your momentum, checking progress against your goals and creating the life you want. Here are some questions to ask yourself when you pause to reflect:

1. What are my top three goals for this week, month or year?

2. On a scale of 1–10 how am I doing against those goals?
3. From whom do I need support for those goals?
4. What new habits have I developed?
5. What habits do I still need to improve?

Write down your answers and then make a calendar note to come back to them in one month, six months or longer. Building accountability into your reflection strengthens it and moves it from daydreaming and musing into a life plan with goals and milestones.

A coaching client of mine, who had recently transitioned from a senior role in government to the private sector, took herself off for a solo overnight to think about the future. She approached this much like a senior management team would do in having an off-site meeting at a nice location to discuss strategy and direction of a company. She applied the same rules: no additional guests, nice location, focus on issues at hand and long-term planning. Her goal was to assess how the transition was going. She was constructing a portfolio career and had recently signed a contract with a major broadcaster and had a number of other offers she needed to consider.

The overnight was very beneficial she said. She had never forced herself to take time out like that to consider where she was headed in her life. She relaxed as well and enjoyed some good food and exercise. She said it was like a mini corporate retreat, but for her life, not a business. On some level, she was astounded that although she had given many, many hours of her professional life to planning the future of organizations for which she had worked, she had never done it for her own future.

Those Whimpering Voices

Not everyone will be happy with you making changes to your life. There are plenty of people in your life who like things the way they are and you the way you are.

Even people who love you and believe they have your best interests at heart are often subconsciously invested in you being the person they know, rather than becoming someone new.

You have to block out their voices if you want to create the life you want.

Courage

As you set out on your journey to create the life you want, equip yourself with as much support as you can. Make it as easy as possible for you to succeed. Take advice sparingly, from people who are wise and want you to be successful. Build habits and routines that make it easier for you to build momentum and be less reliant on willpower. Give yourself time for reflection, renewal and rest. Surround yourself with like-minded spirits. Be courageous in seizing control of your life and living it as you would like. Make a conscious choice to have fun and enjoy the process, even the difficult parts. You will not pass this way again. Why not make it fun and rewarding?

As you move forward, look out for future books from me on the topics of *The Company of the Future: Leadership Skills for Turbulent Times* and *The Portfolio Life: Nailing the Transition from C-Suite to the Board and Beyond.*

NOTES

Chapter 1

1. Martin E.P. Seligman, *Flourish: A Visionary New Understanding of Happiness and Well-being* (Atria Books, 2012).
2. Malcolm Gladwell, *David and Goliath: Underdogs, Misfits, and the Art of Battling Giants* (Little, Brown and Company, 2013).

Chapter 2

1. Robert Fritz, *The Path of Least Resistance for Managers*, 1st ed. (Berrett-Koehler, 1999).
2. W.H. Murray, *The Himalayan Expedition* (1951).
3. Wolfgang Von Goethe, *Faust* (Penguin Classics, 2005).
4. Daniel Gilbert, *Stumbling on Happiness* (Vintage, 2007).

Chapter 3

1. Daniel Kahneman, *Thinking Fast and Slow* (Farrar, Straus and Giroux, 2011).
2. Malcolm Gladwell, *Outliers* (Little, Brown and Company, 2008).
3. Angela Duckworth, *Grit: The Power of Passion and Perseverance* (Scribner, 2016).

4. Carol S. Dweck, *Mindset: The New Psychology of Success* (Ballantine Books, 2007).

5. Francois Voltaire, *Philosophical Dictionary* (Penguin Classics, 1984).

6. Winston Churchill, The International Churchill Society, www.winstonchurchill.org.

7. Robert Watson Watt, *Three Steps to Victory: A Personal Account by Radar's Greatest Pioneer* (Odhams Press Ltd., 1957).

8. Academy of Medical Royal Colleges, *Exercise: The Miracle Cure and the Role of the Doctor in Promoting It* (February 2015).

9. Juvenal, *Sixteen Satires* (Penguin Classics, 1999).

10. Srini Pillay, "Neuroscience Can Help You Live a Healthier Life," *Harvard Health Blog*, Harvard Health Publications, Harvard Medical School, February 29, 2016).

11. J. D. Creswell et al., "Alterations in Resting-State Functional Connectivity Link Mindfulness Meditation With Reduced Interleukin-6: A Randomized Controlled Trial," *Journal of Biological Psychiatry* 80 (July 2016): 53–61.

12. Gretchen Reynolds, "How Meditation Changes the Brain and Body," *The New York Times*, February 18, 2016.

13. www.headspace.com

Chapter 4

1. Charles Duhigg, *The Power of Habit: Why We Do What We Do in Life and Business* (Random House, 2004).

2. Maxwell Malz, *The New Psycho-Cybernetics* (TarcherPerigee, 2015).

Chapter 5

1. John Helliwell, Richard Layard, and Jeffrey Sachs (eds.), *World Happiness Report 2016* (Update, Vol. I). (Sustainable Development Solutions Network, 2016).
2. Paula England, Asaf Levanon, and Paul Allison, "Occupational Feminization and Pay: Assessing Causal Dynamics Using 1950–2000 U.S. Census Data," *Oxford Journals* 88, no. 2: 865–891.
3. Valentina Zarya, "The Percentage of Female CEOs in the Fortune 500 Drops to 4%," *Fortune Magazine*, June 6, 2016.
4. Occupational Feminization and Pay.
5. Pamela Druckerman, "The Perpetual Panic of American Parenthood," *The New York Times*, October 13, 2016.
6. Laura Addati, Naomi Cassirer, and Katherine Gilchrist, *Maternity and Paternity at Work: Law and Practice Across the World* (International Labor Organization, 2014).
7. Ripa Rashid and Sylvia Ann Hewlett, *Winning the War for Talent in Emerging Markets: Why Women Are the Solution* Harvard Business Press, 2013).
8. Anu Partanen, *The Nordic Theory of Everything* ().
9. Daniel Gilbert, *Stumbling on Happiness* (Vintage, 2007).
10. Martin E. P. Seligman, *Flourish: A Visionary New Understanding of Happiness and Well-being* (Atria Books, 2012).

Chapter 6

1. Robert Mankoff, *How About Never—Is Never Good for You?: My Life in Cartoons* (Henry Holt and Company, 2014).
2. Google, "Ten Things We Know to Be True," www.google.com.

Chapter 7

1. Ernest Hemingway, *A Moveable Feast* (Scribner, 2010).

Chapter 8

1. *Downton Abbey*, "Episode Two." Series 1. Directed by Ben Bolt. Written by Julian Fellowes. ITV, September 26, 2010.
2. Bertrand Russell, *In Praise of Idleness: And Other Essays* (Vol. 46) (Routledge Classics, 2004).
3. Ibid.
4. Lucy Kellaway, "January Is for Cutting Down on Long Hours, Not Alcohol," *Financial Times*, January 24, 2016.
5. Amit Kumar, Matthew A. Killingsworth, and Thomas Gilovich, "Waiting for Merlot: Anticipatory Consumption of Experiential and Material Purchases," *Psychological Science*, August 21, 2014.
6. Ibid.
7. James Hamblin, "Buy Experiences, Not Things," *The Atlantic*, October 7, 2014.
8. Ernst & Young, *Shifting from Consumption to Experience: Winning in the Omnichannel Retailing* (2014).
9. Mazda Adli, "Urban Stress and Mental Health," *LSECities*, November 2011.
10. Gregory N. Bratman, Gretchen C. Daily, Benjamin J. Levy, and James J. Gross, "The Benefits of Nature Experience: Improved Affect and Cognition," *Landscape and Urban Planning* 138 (June 2015): 41–50.
11. Wallace Nicholls, *Blue Mind: The Surprising Science That Shows How Being Near, In, On, or Under Water Can Make You Happier, Healthier, More Connected, and Better at What You Do* (Back Bay Books, 2015).

Chapter 9

1. Colin Powell, *Kids Need Structure* TED Talk, January 2013.
2. David Brooks, "The Life Report" and "The Life Report II," *The New York Times*, October 27 and November 28, 2011, respectively.
3. Daniel Gilbert, *Stumbling on Happiness* (Vintage, 2007).
4. Richard Thaler and Cass Sunstein, *Nudge: Improving Decisions About Health, Wealth, and Happiness* (Penguin Books, 2009).
5. Marshall Goldsmith, *Be a Better Leader, Be More Like Your Heroes!*, at www.marshallgoldsmith.com.

Chapter 10

1. L. F. Berkman and S. L. Syme, "Social Networks, Host Resistance and Mortality: A Nine-Year Follow-Up Study of Alameda County Residents," *American Journal of Epidemiology* 109 (1979): 186–204.
2. John Robbins, *Healthy at 100* (Ballantine Books, 2007).
3. Katie Hafner, "Researchers Confront an Epidemic of Loneliness," *The New York Times*, September 5, 2016.
4. Emily Dickinson, "The Loneliness One dare not sound," Emily Dickinson Archive (http://www.edickinson.org/), 1863/1955.
5. Katie Hafner, "Researchers Confront an Epidemic of Loneliness," *The New York Times*, September 5, 2016.
6. The Bible, King James Version, Acts 20:35.
7. Elizabeth W. Dunn, Lara B. Aknin, and Michael I. Norton, "Prosocial Spending and Happiness: Using Money to Benefit Others Pays Off," *Current Directions in Psychological Science* 23 (2014): 41.
8. Michael Lewis, *The Undoing Project: A Friendship That Changed Our Minds* (W. W. Norton & Company, 2016).

9. Lisa Feldman Barrett "Youthful Brains in Older Adults: Preserved Neuroanatomy in the Default Mode and Salience Networks Contributes to Youthful Memory in Superaging," *The Journal of Neuroscience*, September 2015.

Chapter 11

1. Websters Dictionary
2. www.theodore-roosevelt.com/trsorbonnespeech.html
3. McKinsey and Company, *The Power of Many: Realizing the Socioeconomic Potential of Entrepreneurs in the 21st Century*, October 2011.
4. Jeffrey Sparshott, "Sputtering Startups Weigh on U.S. Economic Growth," *The Wall Street Journal*, October 23, 2016.
5. Ibid.
6. Isaac Newton, *Principia Mathematica Philosophiae Naturalis* (referenced by NASA at website grc.nasa.gov).

INDEX

Index